CAVIAR LITERATURE

GASTON CAVALLERI

Copyright © Caviar Literature LLC, 2015
First published in 2015 by Caviar Literature LLC
www.caviarliterature.com

Author: Gaston Cavalleri.
Title: Blue Smartie / G. Cavalleri.
ISBN: 978-0-9873045-9-9 (eBook)
ISBN: 978-0-9873045-8-2 (Paperback)

Blue Smartie

GASTON CAVALLERI

Acknowledgements

Nan, thank you so much for everything you ever did for me. Thanks for getting up and making my porridge, cup of tea and baked beans on toast every morning for six years, when I was a crazy teenager.

Grandpa, thanks for being my dad, my mate and for giving me my proud ways. Thanks for teaching me to be real.

Mum, thanks for teaching me how to be a survivor, from the start, and then later saving my arse in this world.

All three parents have been a perfect recipe.

Author's note

The purpose of this book was to prepare people who have never had unlimited freedom for the roads that follow if they ever find themselves on the path of it. People spend their entire lives wishing for freedom, but never prepare for the day it arrives. I had no intention to do wrong by anybody, in any way, while writing this story. Character names and anniversary dates have been changed in the story to protect anybody who might coincidentally lead a life similar to that of any characters I depict in the narrative.

Blue Smartie

Blue Smartie

Contents

Preface

A person can hear people say, "You should write a book," only so many times before acting. When I decided it was time to write *Blue Smartie*, I was 31 and had been travelling for 32 months. I'd been all over the world in search of a home away from my country, and one that had Latin features. For some reason, I'd been escaping the English-speaking world.

I did most of my writing in a small apartment in Medellin, Colombia, over five months, reflecting on life and more recent events. I'd done bits and pieces throughout my travels, but in Colombia I was completely alone, and due to the cultural differences, not too many people wanted to hear the products of my wacky mind.

When I originally sat down to write my story, I needed to come to terms with some of the events that'd evidently affected my mind. I believe that everything happens for a reason and that we sometimes experience low times so we can smile when the high times arrive. I ain't a sorry, sad, "poor me" kinda guy, I can assure you; even though everything that's happened in my life has been at the extreme "up" or "down" end of the spectrum, I've been lucky enough to find a laugh throughout the entire ride.

The thing is, by the time I arrived in Colombia I had many things on my mind, and in South America it wouldn't always be wisest to share my story with everyone I met. I mean, some of those people have serious problems, such as not having shoes or food—and plenty bloody more; that's for sure. Everybody has a story, and some people have an extreme one; it was just that I had stuff I needed to get off my chest, and I'd never seen a "shrink," so I thought I'd have a crack at sorting the stuff out myself.

You see, sometimes when you're sharing a story like mine, people can't see how it's a problem—and it's not, either, I must say. The problem lies more in the changes in the people around you after you tell them your details. The changes can manifest in various ways; it's just that as time goes on, the story plays on the human mind.

I'm living an interesting life and one that's very different from the lives of a lot of people who are caught up in the rat race or their society. I've been lucky enough to be able to escape being caught up, for now. I understand that circumstances can change at any point in a person's life and that, as a consequence, we should never take anything for granted. I found that out while sitting in a hospital bed about a year and a half ago, when I'd gone a little too loco at Brazil's Carnival. I got flown home in a wheelchair, was operated on and found out what it's like to be without physical function for a bit. Everything happens for a reason.

Now I've got my function back, and I'm well and truly back on my horse, I've been fortunate enough to recognize the importance of my body's functioning, and I've reached the stage at which I need to exercise my mind. Not something you'd usually hear a tough-guy Australian male say, but it's time to evolve and beat the game that society's created. Now's when you either sink or swim.

When you've finished reading the book at hand, please think about the journey and what it's like to be in someone else's shoes. Some people will pinch the eye out of your dick, if you're not looking. The problem for them isn't their short-term gain; it's what they'll gain in the end.

Blue Smartie

Cheers,

Gaston

1

Pikey

Good old Macquarie Fields—I wonder what's happening in that place at the moment; it's nice to be out of there. I still recall the day my old lady carried me into our home there in 1981; I was a rubbery age of one—born January 18th the previous year. She was carrying me on her shoulder to inspect a shitty little fibro, government-funded white and brown box; brand spanking new, as it was still without carpet. My eyes gazed bleakly, as I dangled face-down in her arms. I was observing the uncovered pine floor, feeling frightened by the scattered wooden knots in each plank as I thought they were hundreds of monsters' eyes, each of them pulsating and glaring at me. I'd burst into tears and my twenty-year-old mother began to bounce me on her hip, while a government lady showed us around our new home. For the next seven years this was the place I called home.

The street was full of rogues, and so were the neighboring streets of our less-than-classy suburb; the area was full of desperate people, from broken families that a capitalist might refer to as trash. I don't know why my mother was attracted to that sort of environment, but she always was, and that attraction resulted in some real deadbeat boyfriends. It seemed to be one dirt bag followed by another. One of these lowlifes ended up being the father of my sister, and my actual father, another character, was a piece of crap too. I can't say I recall him around as a young boy, which probably explains why we were accepting a government-funded home before I could walk.

They say that in all bad things there's a little bit of good and in all good things there's a little bit of bad; after the life I've seen I believe it's a decision to opt for your route.

At four years old I learned that my grandfather had been shot in the head by an organized hit. He ran a "truck" business that I'd visited as a young child, getting my hands covered in grease and witnessing groups of men roaming around his truck depot.

"He's too young to go to the funeral," Mum said after he was killed.

I'm still curious to this day who was there. I didn't even know what death or a murder meant back then; there weren't many in the cartoons I was watching. I was struggling to interpret "father"—let alone "grandfather"— so joining the dots to my grandfather's murder was complex.

"You don't want to know about him," my mother's father said. "He did the wrong thing, and somebody killed him."

The hit-man was on the run for around ten years after the murder. There was a show on television in the 80s called *Australia's Most Wanted* that provided me with my family history in the comfort of my own home. As a young kid, sitting beside your toys finding out that you're watching a television program with actors reproducing the murder of own grandfather, when you barely know your father, I have to say, is an experience that teaches you that *shit happens*—and there's no point crying over spilt milk.

At least I wasn't the one who was shot.

"What do you know about the murder of...?" An investigator asked the hit-man, adding my grandfather's name.

"I know about it," replied the murderer. "I shot him." He raises his index finger to the middle of forehead. "Right there. The bullet got him right between the eyes." The tone was cold. Then he added, "Must've been about to enjoy a seafood platter; there was a seafood basket left on the table."

They found the killer in 1994. He'd done other murders in Australia in the 80s and he's now considered one of a group of five of the most dangerous people in Australia. He's sitting in a cell in the super-max prison in Goulburn—home to Australia's deadliest killers.

Should I go and see this character, see how he's going in his prison cell? I've thought. Then I snap. *Why would you want to open up that tin of worms?*

Around the time of the murder, I rarely saw my old man—not that I recall seeing him even a handful of times before. I was four when the murder happened—my father left my mother before I turned one.

My old man's relationship with his father wasn't great; he was considered a suspect in the murder, since the man contracted to do the hit was on the run. If my father didn't disappear he could've been the subject of the next hit.

Crime had a deteriorating effect on that side of the family. After the murder I'd visited the grandfather's house—it was tense. The house was a double story home, decorated with shotguns in different rooms, behind doors and various other locations in the building. A handful of men were there, as small televisions, with cameras hooked up to them, monitored outside the house.

My brother was six years old, two years older than me. He was considered more responsible by our father, "If anybody ever comes to the house," my father said, shaking a shotgun near his head. "You go and get this for daddy from behind the door." He looked at my brother as he fed a thumb-sized red and gold bullet into a barrel. "You put the bullet in here like this."

"I wanna get it," I cried. "Why can't I get it for you?"

"Be quiet. You're too young."

"A bad tin of worms," was a chapter title in a book I once read. It was about Australian crime and referred to my grandfather's truck business illegally transporting drugs in trailers between states. There were references to organized killings and big money—none of which I ever saw. I know this because my mother was always a single battling woman, as broke as could be in Australia. I was shown the book by my mother's mother. "When that family began, a bad tin of worms was opened," she said.

Many criminal events became public on my father's side. My mother's family kept this from me, fearing it would corrupt my "bad tin of worms" mind. I just wanted know who I was without hearing it from the mouths of others who'd learned it from newspapers, televisions and murders.

Finding my own way was a shaky learning curve. I recall a day I was in the kitchen in Macquarie Fields, searching the cupboard for black-and-white labeled tins of beans to hear the slap of knuckles smacking a jaw followed by teeth snapping against teeth. I could see, out of the corner of my eye, that the thug of a father of the girl who was soon to be my new sister had punched some bloke in the head. This man hadn't been in my world for long, and I'm certain the knuckle slapping was about nothing entrepreneurial. Nonetheless, it was entertainment at home; I was so excited. As a kid, I'd always watched fights at my local public school; to have one at home was a real treat. At the time, I was a very observant five-year-old and thought: *For as tough as this guy thinks he is, I thought he'd hit harder than that.*

This was my new fill in father, who'd just shown me, that if things didn't go my way I could defer to my five-year-old logic.

Most people who lived in the area were nothing but unfortunate. One big family on our street stood out like a bee sting. They occupied a few of the fibro homes on our block, with a crew of these family members living right next door to us. They were an unbelievably wild family who never had a dull moment. There was always action with this crew: anything from keeping guns and stealing, to using bows and arrows. In one case, one of them, I'm afraid to say, even laid a turd on the neighbors' doorstep and pissed in their windows. They talk about the "tall poppy syndrome" in Australia and this was a classic case of it.

It was a housing commission street with a neighbor who'd managed to purchase his home. You'd see the owner watering and tending his garden. The housing-commission neighbors didn't want this attraction to fly too high, so, soon after, a turd was laid on his porch and a neatly trimmed tree was dowsed in petrol, then set on fire. As for the villains involved in the man's misery, I know they've experienced unfortunate events in life—one is now dead, and others have seen the inside of a jail.

It was a bit sad, really. I don't know why I say they didn't have an opportunity, because they were in a great country; they just seemed destined for bad things. Everything they did that I think about was heading to a bad place. I'm not even going to think about what's happening to that family now, and I don't plan on following it up, either.

I remember when one of the family members, a mate of mine, was electrocuted. He was nine, poor little bugger, and I was eight. He was just mucking around, as a wild kid would without supervision, and somehow found himself interested in an enormous electricity substation that a section of Macquarie Fields got its power from. As it turned out, one fence wasn't enough to keep this little man from exploring the plant, and *zap*: dead nine weeks later. There was a public swimming pool beside the station. The story goes that his seven-year-old brother dragged him, as he burned from the voltage, to the swimming pool to put the body's flames out in the water. Apparently the woman at the turnstile entrance passed out when she saw the young body arrive. The water was how he bought his remaining nine weeks. And what was his last wish? To see a national skateboard champ—these are pretty simple people who enjoyed simple pleasures.

Kids used to run wild in the streets of our area. It wasn't possible for parents to know where their kids were. From what I could tell back then, most of the parents were alcoholics, and unfortunately, that form of childcare often had consequences.

I nearly had a premature good-bye a couple of years earlier. I was messing around in a dirty, dark river in Macquarie Fields while all the parents were on the piss. The river was as dirty and unclear as can be. The desolate bush land near the river always had an eerie feeling. I recall exploring the water, and next thing I knew, I'd gone under as a result of a pothole at the river bottom. I was below the dark water and beginning to drown—good fun as a five-year-old. I'd given up my attempt at paddling to the surface, remembering that I wasn't able to swim. I hadn't yet discovered the fear of death. I could see the sun shining down from the water's surface, spanning rays out on me as I sank deeper—struggling for air, looking up to the sun; *nobody knows I'm here.* I went still. I gulped for oxygen. I felt myself sinking and fading away. Then, I was swept out of the river. *My mum did have an eye on me!* I was stuffed if I knew she was even there. I guess my peripheral vision still hadn't developed, but more importantly, I'm glad she found me. She would've been distraught at losing me; she'd already lost one of my brothers an hour after his birth. She jumped in with all her clothes on, and I remember her breathing heavily—seeming both grateful and shocked.

About a week after that incident, my good friend, a little Aboriginal girl, drowned in the same spot. My mother broke the news to me. I can imagine it'd been a similar scenario—parents on the piss. She was one year younger, so let's face it, at that age, that sort of thing requires real supervision. Anyway, the poor girl was dead, and a search team found her about a week later, wedged under a log in the river. We never saw much of her mother after that. I'd usually gotten dropped off at her housing-commission home, and her single mother would keep an eye on me and her daughter, who was the first girl who was my friend. I suppose her mother didn't want to watch me, or be reminded of me, after her death. That wasn't so clear to me then.

There always seemed to be something tragic happening back in those days. I guess you could say I was lucky; I got to look and learn. There were plenty of kids unsupervised and able to get away with murder. The street we lived on formed a small *cul de sac* and was well known to the local police. There was always some sort of domestic violence scene or neighbor dispute followed by a police visit.

The place was full of Australian pikeys—hopeless whites living on social security. They lived in government housing and the street was always chock-a-block—nobody ever worked. All the pikeys had plenty of kids, and they were all about the same age. I think it was them, and young single mothers, who generally needed social housing.

An ice-cream man occasionally cruised round the block, trying to flog things off to the kids. He stopped coming after a while. There were so many unsupervised kids mucking around on skateboards. The kids used to get on the back of the poor guy's van with their skateboards and hang on for dear life, and I must say I was one of them.

"One of the kids from another street got run over," Mum told me, about the same time that the ice-cream man's visits to our street decreased. No major drama with me, since I never got an ice-cream. This could have also contributed to the decrease in the visits. I doubt any of the kids in that street got ice-creams.

Cracker Night was a big event on the block. We used to make a blazing big bonfire, or at least the older kids did. It was on the waste ground close to the homes. When the waste ground wasn't used for a bonfire everybody usually played football or Bull Rush—similar to Rugby League, but without the ball. There was no tennis back then; all the pikeys were total Neanderthals, and heaven help you if you were a little pansy. At least that was the image tennis had back then. Looking back and comparing to now, tennis would be the sport of choice for me.

The bonfires were good until everybody started tossing fireworks in them and aiming bangers at each other. The whole Cracker Night theme was canned by the government because kids started getting serious burns from jumping jacks hitting them. Interesting how people can stuff things up. The whole point of the theme was to celebrate the Queen's birthday—congratulations: let's shoot each other with bangers, get completely pissed and start bashing each other the English way. Of course, any pikey gathering wouldn't be complete without a fight, and that was always the case among parents attending the gathering.

13

I recall going to a Sunday school when I was young—as a three-year-old, walking but still crapping my pants. During that time, some man came to hang around my brother and I after school. The guy never paid too much attention to me. I didn't know why he should've; I just remember seeing Mum trying to force him my way.

During that meeting, he didn't hang around too long, and the only thing I remember from it is a packet of sugar for a takeaway coffee. I hadn't even registered that he was my father. I didn't know at that age that I needed a father. I didn't register I was supposed to have two parents until my mother forced me to phone my "father."

I've got one of those? I was slightly surprised.

A short while into the phone call I discovered the prick wasn't keen on talking.

I was three and had little clue. Mum just said: "Ring your dad and tell him you miss him."

I didn't know I missed him until then.

Kids get shy on the phone with anybody. I didn't know who this guy was I was supposed to tell, "I miss you."

Mum sat beside me while I called and said "Tell him that all the other kids at school had a father and I didn't."

Stuff me . . . that's true!

This was the first time I realized it.

If you told a kid that everybody had chocolate at school and you didn't have it, you'd better be ready for the shit to hit the fan, 'cause it would.

I cried until I forgot, and never really thought about it until I was reminded again. I'd say that'd be typical of life for a young pikey kid. It's not that bad, not having a father during the years when you have no idea; you just need to be saved by having some guidance at some point, and that point has to be before it's all too late.

I remember those old days, hanging out on that government-funded street. During a similar time, not long after that call to my father, my old girl clearly began drowning her sorrows. She drowned them like a frantic young girl would with 23 years round her neck. This provided some of my entertainment as a young kid, since it meant that she'd hang out at the local no-hopers' pub, which was full of the worst kind of humans—a center for all the social misfits on benefits. Anybody who wound up there of his own accord was useless. I can understand why the single women with kids wound up there: it must be hard trying to live life alone with dependants—although, you'd have to ask why they chose to hang out in such a terrible pub.

They'd all sit around that dump drowning their sorrows from the mess they'd gotten themselves into. It was clear that none of the younger women there would've had any parenting support from wiser relatives trying to warn them about their situation—at least in the case of those who had relatives. If fathers had had a little more presence, and done a little more, I don't believe those girls would've let just any lowlife cozy up to them.

We moved away from that street after living in it for seven years. Mum had met my sister's father, and I guess we were always destined to move out of there. Mum wasn't stupid; she knew Macquarie Fields was a rough place to raise kids. She didn't know how to get out of there alone, and needed male support. After experiencing years of fights, stealing and children's deaths in that area, once Mum found support to move, she got herself out of there, and we kids got the hell out with her.

From there, we brushed through Warwick Farm. Not even sure why we moved there; we didn't even have a house. We moved in with this ginger friend of Mum's. She had a government house on the corner of a street. That didn't last more than two weeks. This woman was a single pikey mother who smoked like a chimney and had a few pikey kids of her own.

While I was there, I was enrolled in a new school for a couple of weeks and played the new kid for that time. This was the same story in government schools in the poorer areas: get picked on until you bash the tough kid. That stops you being bullied any more. I did that, then we were back on the road.

From there we moved back to the country—to Tamworth—only this time, it was without a house. I think Mum thought she'd get help from my grandad, but because her new, soon-to-be "Father of the Year" boyfriend was from a different culture and didn't work, that idea didn't sit so well with my grandad's old-fashioned ways.

Grandpa had been to three wars, and believed he knew a bit about people as a result, and saw this new

17

character, who his daughter was settling with, as nothing more than an uneducated, unemployed bum whose life included growing up in a broken Maori family in New Zealand. He'd already fathered children he had no contact with—it wasn't rocket science. His outlook would've been completely different from a young girl's from out in the sticks. You need to consider all the variables: if my grandad couldn't see that this pair had no future … Well, I'm stuffed if I know how he ended up being right. As a human, there are certain signs you can pick up on to find out a bit about people—kind of like when the clouds come and it rains shortly after.

Anyway, since Grandpa had a small farm outside of town and a caravan, that was us for a bit. Happy days: we were travelers. I found myself in a new school in Tamworth, with the weight of seven years round my neck—and living in a caravan like a trailer park carnie. We'd parked the caravan up against a small shed on the farm. A decent storm would've blown it over. In fact, years later, one did. There was no power or plumbing rigged up to the site. The galvanized shed was put there to store tools and bales of hay. A bucket was positioned in another small galvanized shack with a toilet seat on it—this increased the star rating as this was our lavatory. The shack was without light and about one meter square—not too flash for taking a dump, forever worrying if a red back spider would creep out from under the seat and tickle your backside. But this was the least of the worries: at least you wouldn't get your bum wet, as the bucket was without water waiting for the drop. Emptying that thing was the only thing I can think of that the new dad was doing well.

The 1970s caravan that was parked beside the shed wasn't too flash either. Luckily, this form of living wasn't to last too long. How this circumstance even crossed the mind of my acting parents is beyond me. We soon moved up in the world—to the local caravan park. Now, I was a proper carnie ... A carnie on a farm? Come on: carnies live with carnies.

I was enrolled in a school during a two-week period and my mother told me that I needed to keep the caravan scenario a secret from the people at school. I couldn't see the issue. To me, I thought we were camping, just that it was full-time. This park traveler scenario lasted four weeks. We moved to the other side of town, and I was in another new school and housing-commission home. I'd just finished playing the new kid at school; this was a shame 'cause it was too soon to be fighting young playground standover men again.

We lived in a little estate with other government-funded homes, full of people who weren't so lucky. This was just for a short stint... Mum and the "Father of the Year" had already begun to have problems. My stay in the country came crashing down ... there I was back to the good old streets of Sydney, except this time, my little sister was on the way and we found ourselves living in a government box in Western Sydney. Mum had tracked this down in no time. In fact we seemed to do better with the "Father of the Year" now around less. I guess the government needed to watch out for Mum, because on paper, she was a single mum of two with a bun in the oven. Tough gig, if you ask me.

At least we were out of Macquarie Fields and into Miller. Another rough area, but I'd have to say, better than Mac Fields. It had a different type of local—not so much the pikey-English type; more the new immigrants and refugees, with a sprinkling of pikeys.

Mum put me into a new school, and a funny little one at that. I don't know what would've become of some of those little characters. There were some nice kids there— we had an Emad, a Mohammad and a Mustafa, and they were pretty regular names. We also had a Wayne, a Shayne and a Wally, and all the other beautiful English names. There was a Huyliem and a Ho, just to add a touch of the Oriental. It was an interesting multicultural concoction in a government-funded community. I can't talk bad about any of those people—none of them, or us, had a chance to live anywhere else. I hope they all had as much luck as I had—those fibro-clad houses were bloody terrible.

I know more now, though, and even the lowest quality of housing in Australia is a lot better than the lowest in Brazil, Argentina or Colombia, and many other countries are much worse off. I'm grateful that, even though I thought I was hard done by, in reality, I was still doing well. A lot of people in Colombia would love the opportunity to have babies and get paid to send them to school like the people in Australia's government-funded communities.

Looking back on the past, and to now have my degree and seem to be a nearly "normal" person, is a real treat for me. At least I think I seem normal; I'm not too sure whether that's the truth.

Sometimes, people look at me funny. I'm not sure what they think. I can only guess. Maybe they just can't make me out. I was dragged through the dirt but have still managed to now do what "normal" people tend to do: I've got a university degree, I've done more travel than many people, and it's all unbelievable for me. The only people who'd do more traveling than I do would be the filthy rich—whatever that means—and I don't even know what they'd have to do to be doing more travel.

Maybe I'm not so creative in the end; I just know how to get on planes to go to live in foreign countries. Maybe others with cash jump out of planes and climb huge mountains with all top-shelf clothes, and have big backpacks full of classy traveling things that'd soon get robbed anyway in some of the countries that offer the most fun.

Some of those people I'm trying to work out are obviously trying to work me out, judging by the dazed looks they give me from time to time.

"You haven't seen half the shit that I've seen," I was told a few years back, by a man who considered he'd received a raw deal in life.

I'll take that as a compliment; he thinks I look normal.

People make assumptions about others. They assume that because somebody's bought nice clothes, on special, that they must be doing ok.

I had a "best" friend once who couldn't seem to stay composed when he discovered my mother had bumped into some cash. He was from a comfortable family in the country and had hard-working parents. I would've thought he'd be happy for me ... We were so close during our senior school years. I suppose some people start to feel green when they discover they don't have something up on you. I had no idea people thought like that; I was always used to having less than everybody, and accepted it, so never knew the feeling of having more than anybody. I think when there are bigger problems, such as somebody else has a father and you don't, as a kid, things like

23

somebody's family having a nicer car or bigger house are just issues that you're used to.

When people find, or their imagination tells them, that you have more, and then think, *Perhaps this guy's got it up on me*—or at least that's what the voice in their head says—they must start feeling fragile. I have no idea, but there's definitely a change in the air when less fortunate people find out. I find the luckier people are in life the less they seem to mind. When I do see that change in air, that's often close to the end of my connection with that person.

When I think back to the old streets with me and the screaming kids, the fact we had little supervision probably doesn't seem so bad to me. What's perfect, after all? It could be said that a lot of the kids who play alone learn to survive alone. There are a lot of problems with learning alone, though, or should I say risks? I don't think it's a planned activity for a lot of the families in the old street to have their kids running wild; it was an out of control situation full of broken families. I can only pluck positives from it as I was saved in the end.

I'd say a lot of those kids would be in bad spots now. I've mentioned two who died. It would be a bad dream to imagine how their parents must feel. I was told that one of them received a financial pay out for the mishap, but money can't replace a soul.

There were some crazy kids on that street and I'm surprised it was just two of my little friends who passed away. Some of the kids in the street found access to their parents' stored weapons so it's a wonder further accidents didn't result.

At five years old, I recall I was at my neighbors' home—he was older than me, about 14 at the time— and he was pointing a bow and arrow at me, point blank. He thought it was funny to have an arrow fully cocked and directly against my chest. He watched me near soiling my pants while hiding myself under a kitchen chair. I didn't want to let him know I was scared, but I was clearly not having fun.

His oldies were alkies. They weren't bad people—or at least I thought not, back then. They treated you as family. If you were one of them, you were one of them. Having said that, somebody flogged my brother's and my pushbikes one weekend when we'd gone to see the grandparents, and that family were originally considered to be suspects. We, as kids, were made to think so for some time.

The bikes were taken even though a couple of good dogs were in the yard. My so-called old man had done a one-off and just bought them for my brother and me. Looking back, the real suspect would've been the good-for-nothing boyfriend my mother had. I'd say he flogged them and sent them to the pawnshop.

This is like taking candy from a baby—or a bicycle from a five-year-old.

It's funny how people can affect you. I didn't have anything to do with that, I was just trying to be a kid and enjoy a present from my phantom father. It would've been difficult for the neighbors to take the bikes; they would've been ripped up by our dogs. There were two bikes, so that's two trips. Stuff that from the perspective of a young, robbing teenager. They were just bikes ... But that dodgy boyfriend of my mother's was always up to something. If it wasn't fighting some silly bum down the pub, it was stealing and hiding something—or hiding himself. He was clearly good for nothing. That's all grandad was warning the old girl of. Poor bloke really let that get out of his hands.

I had the most respect for my grandad you could ever have for a person. I think this is due to the fact he raised me in the end. He got me through my teenage years. It wasn't his job, but he stepped up for it. Not only did he raise me; he put everything into the job. He didn't take too many shortcuts in bringing me up. That's why I love him. What he did for me, he did with passion. This was the difference between me and those kids running wild in the streets—I was saved. Grandpa could see all that leading to bad places.

With age, I'd say, you see things differently. You see things before they arrive. I consider myself very lucky; I've seen it from both sides. I know what it's like to be a little bastard with nothing. You don't know it's that bad when you're young and in it. But you sense something's not right, especially when you don't know where the old man is, or why the prick won't put his hand up for the job.

If it wasn't for the useless old man, the problems would never have been there. He used to work hard— well, as far as I knew, he did. I believed he was driving trucks long distance between states. All his family drove trucks—they messed around with semi-trailers, or at least that's what I thought. How hard could it've been to sort a bit of money aside to feed your kids? I'd say he'd still be running from the Child Support Agency chasing him for maintenance these days—under a different name, for that or whatever reason.

I hope all those other little buggers from the street are doing okay. It was never their fault; they had useless parents.

2

Country bumpkin

Before better times, as kids, my brother and I used to visit the grandparents' house in the country. Those times were pretty good, and I looked forward to them a lot. My grandfather treated my brother and me as his own children, and probably better.

He didn't get too much luck, my old grandad; I mean, he did, but the son he hoped would carry his family name died as a teenager—Uncle Daniel, on the 13th of November 1980. Grandpa had served in three wars, fighting for his family and country, and to have his name stop at him was not something that sat well. My grandmother was a little lady from Malta, and acted like one, and supported my grandfather as a proud man who worked hard, put food on the table and paid for their home.

Grandpa was there to help the family, and helping's what he thought he was doing by stepping in and assisting my mother to raise my brother and me. My mother was his eldest daughter. She never really got along with her siblings.

After years of witnessing my brother's and my situation, my grandfather ended up stepping in, and our visits to the grandparents' house became permanent living. Grandpa loved his daughter and us, and couldn't bear to witness our family falling to pieces. Even after everything that's happened to me, I consider this hand to be the luckiest, life-changing event in my life. I couldn't see any problems emerging from my grandfather's love, being an 11-year-old when the move happened; I just wanted as much family as I could get at the time.

Thanks to my education with my grandad during the senior school years while I was living with him, I learnt to be a very honorable man. He taught me so much and put everything into me, as he did for my brother, although I can only speak for myself. He treated us as another chance at having sons. He did everything, and minus nothing, for us, and for some reason this raised issues for onlookers. It was clear that Grandpa had a new energy. My brother and I just thought *that's Grandpa's way*. We loved him so much for what he was doing. I'd never felt loved before then; it was a new feeling. Growing up with my mother before then was different; Mum wasn't coping so well with the hand she'd been dealt.

I got lucky and was saved by the person who'd become my best friend and my father for the rest of my life. I've never met anybody more straight than my grandfather. He taught me that if somebody didn't like what I was saying, well, I could put my hands up and box. I was just a young guy in the country. It doesn't happen these days. It didn't happen then, either; it was a way of thinking which taught me to never lie: If you don't lie, you don't have petty fights. The only time I had fights as a teenager was when the truth wasn't good enough for somebody. Even back then there were smarter options— but through this attitude, knowing I could always handle the worst scenario, I learnt to be straight with my words.

Grandpa used to love taking me to my sports, and it didn't matter where. I think this is because he lost a sport-loving son. My brother and I were there with a new love I

31

can never forget. Grandpa loved the amusement of having two new crazy sons. He'd get so excited at the simplest teenage stories. One in particular was the story of the "urinator," which was a name I was given by a teacher in Year 9. It was on a Thursday, when I was walking to sport from school, and I needed a leak, so I took one.

While I'm enjoying my piss, a teacher rides past and sees me in school uniform, peeing on a tree. He sees me once, does a double take and nearly falls off his bike. He pulls over and gives me a meeting with the deputy head for the next day. I duly arrived at the deputy head's office.

"Ahhhh, soooo, you're the urinator," the deputy says, upon my arrival.

For some reason, Grandpa loved that final phrase. He'd make me tell it every time he saw me. He had a big grin on his face every time. I have to say I don't see the humor in it; I was just taking a piss—but I'm happy such a simple thing could bring such laughter to my grandad.

For some reason, some people showed signs that they couldn't come to terms with the fact that my Grandpa had simple needs and that those needs were met for him in reality. He was given a second go at having grandkids who loved him. He couldn't just be left to enjoy it. People can be really bitter and spiteful if things don't go their way.

For the next six years, I continued to stay with the grandparents, and endure negative energy from onlookers, who I'd expected to love me. I don't know why the cookie crumbles this way. I'm sorry my mother was having problems and couldn't look after us. My brother and I didn't have much choice but to develop thicker skins and just keep on getting on with what had to be done—finish school and become independent.

Maybe I'd be a spiteful if was incapable of giving life a decent go ... I'd probably need something to blame in life, if that was the case. I couldn't care if I have to take the wrap for my own screw-ups. I think if you're willing to, you've got a better chance of knocking the mistake on the head. I've messed up a lot and every time the problems been with me. Part of screwing up is recognizing how to avoid it the next time; it's more about how you recover.

"Now's when you 'sink' or 'swim,'" my mother use tell me. It was never my style to want somebody else to swim for me, or to make excuses if somebody else was swimming faster. I've seen a lot of the latter, coming originally from poorer areas. I've had the opportunity to live amongst useless people. I've heard nothing but excuses from some of them who don't move forward. The longer they live, the more it becomes evident they're not moving. Eventually, the excuses don't work, and in order to continue living comfortably in their bubble, these people need you to get away—before you pop it.

I saw this with a "good" mate from Tamworth. He was very happy living alongside me when I was broke, living with my grandparents. His bubble was safe. My grandparents were simple people who cared for nothing other than having everybody in the family safe and well.

We'd met because I could play sports very well. That had a lot to do with my internal anger with the world, which was largely related to not having a couple of my very own parents and being at the lower end of the social scale. Sport made things level.

I thought my mate would be happy for me. I never thought he could change. When I told him how lucky I'd been, I had no idea what was going through his mind. I just assumed he'd want the best for me. I felt so comfortable that he'd be glad; I was just in my own world and cried with happiness after I told him. I lay on the street and was as happy as Larry; that was the first moment I'd ever experienced tears of joy.

A few days later, I'm talking to him on the phone and he mentions he's been thinking about what I said to him. I'm wondering what he means, because I don't know what I said to him. For me, it's more what's happened to me—that's what he should've been talking about—but instead, the issue for him's not what's happened to me but what he's heard or what I said to him and how it's affected his bubble.

"Yeah … What?" I say.

"I'm a bit jealous, actually."

"Hey?"

"I'm a bit jealous."

That was another intro into how people can shine. That was the start of the end of that guy. What was I supposed to do? I just got lucky.

Hey, Uncle Daniel,

Hope you're well wherever you are.

I never really thanked you for what you did for me. You watched over and made sure I was safe. You gave me a father at great cost to you. That must've been hard. I know you weren't ready to leave this world. I know you've had a part in my life, and I thank you for the assistance. I hope you're enjoying the show, and I promise I'll always do the right thing by you.

Your parents really looked after me, and I can't express how they changed my life and made me breathe again. The day your father took me under his wing was the day my life changed forever. He saw you in me. I used to see your photo up in the dining room and your sports certificates in the lounge. I guess you did look like me; the family used to say that. They never talked to me about you

36

too much after you died. I think it was something they wanted in the past.

I want to see you one day, and I want you to be proud of the life I've led. I won't let you down, and I thank you again for what you've done for me. You've been a good guide, and you're welcome in my life for as long as you like.

Love,

Gaston

Blue Smartie

3

The Big Smoke

After spending my entire senior school years living with the grandparents, I moved straight back to Sydney. I was still very green, having become a typical country kid. My grandfather had taught me to respect him, and I had absolutely no desire to let him down. It was a completely different scene in the Big Smoke this time around. I was 18 and had no craving to be back in the wilder parts of Sydney.

Actually, I felt rather sick when I was out that way. My mother was still living out there, but in a slightly different area. She'd managed to clean up her life a bit during this time. When I say that, I mean she was still poor, but she just wasn't hanging around such no-hopers; these ones were just harmless alcoholics who couldn't hold a job. This did my head in, but I had to move forward, so I decided never to go out to that neck of the woods. I didn't feel right when I was there, and it reminded me of my past. That was something I didn't want to fall back into, and in order to keep my head clear, I opted to steer well away until I'd moved forward.

I'd been dragged through the gutter and was still keeping on keeping on. I didn't have a qualification or anything, but I was getting pretty qualified for anything that came my way. You get to a point in life where not too much can affect you. You always have to look on the bright side, and at that age—18—I believe that was when this attitude developed in me. I was happy; I'd been loved by that age. After doing my stint living with the grandparents, I felt I had people who cared about me. When I moved out of my grandparents', I felt I'd been born again. I managed to always look on the bright side.

Throughout the years, my grandparents had given me certain sayings I used for living day to day. I thank whoever's responsible, for everything. My grandparents were a present that could never be replaced. My grandfather used to always tell me, "Don't look for trouble; it'll find you." It wasn't a demand, just a suggestion, to indicate he'd been down many roads, and that was the way to go down them.

I never looked for trouble, but sure enough, in my younger years it found me. That was good enough for me; it was just the right dose of trouble. I kind of needed the action, really. I took a great deal of notice of Grandpa's sayings and whatever he'd told me. He didn't just talk for the sake of talking.

A couple of other pointers he gave me throughout the years were: "Men don't argue; women argue; men just let it all boil up inside. Just let it boil up until it's too late. Let it go and go, and then, when you're sure they want to resolve it, you let them have it —you leave the women to argue." Now, some mightn't see the sense in this little piece of wisdom, but things never get to the final stage. If you don't argue, you chill and let it all breeze by.

"Never underestimate your opponent," he'd also say.

Nan had her little list she dropped in from time to time, and it was funny to see a little Maltese lady walking around the house saying those lines she'd clearly learnt in her time.

"Your best friend is your pocket," was one of them. I never really got that one until a few years had gone by and I'd learnt that friends aren't always so close—nor family members, either, for that matter. I interpret the saying now as that your pockets are the closest things to you, and are the only things that'll always be by your side, even if they're empty.

"No money, no honey; no money, no funny." "Money is the root of all evil." "They will borrow your money and even borrow your girlfriends." All strange sayings, for some, but I've found them helpful, along with education, in shaping my views about taking on this world. Sometimes you have to simplify things—get the clouds out of the sky.

I used to talk to my grandad a lot and listen to everything he had to say. As I've said, he just wasn't a man who felt he had to speak all the time; he just said things that had to be said, and without demanding, so I listened.

Nan used to laugh at me. I could see she liked the entertainment of watching me growing up, with my antics. I'm sure she knew exactly what I was up to with everything. My grandfather would've been larking around, growing up, and Nan would've seen all of it and then seen it in me.

When I moved back to Sydney, I used my grandparents' knowledge to help me get through. I still hadn't bumped into cash, and I had no financial help, but I didn't see that as a problem at the time; I thought that was the way things were, and moved on. I couldn't get money from the grandparents because I would've caused jealousy among the family members—and they knew that the way I was going was the way to learn.

I couldn't talk to the old man. Actually, he played games with the old girl's head and told her I wasn't his son. I hadn't seen him for more than 10 years, and even then it was only by accident and for five minutes.

I had a mission to sort out on my own and a relatively clear head, thanks to the love I got from my grandparents. I knew I needed to buy time to think, so I got a little bar job for that purpose.

It was my first bar job, and a funny one. I remember rocking in and asking for a job. There was a good Aussie bloke there, chuffed, I could see, because I was there asking for work. The bar was in an area of Sydney known

43

for rogues. It was the inner city, though, and not back on the outskirts. Those folks were also very multicultural, and there were many clashes because people from the area were proud and not willing to bite their tongues.

People earned money in that area, though; there were some real wheelers and dealers, and it wasn't a bad intro into Sydney life with people who wanted to own things. This was my first crack at proper city living, and the bar job was a way to support it.

The bar had strippers scheduled every Friday evening, and all the local tradesmen attended the shows. There was also a mix of people heading out of Sydney, seeing as the bar was in the city and on a direct route to the southern suburbs.

The bar was owned by a pack of Greek boys, and good for them; they had their things together for the club. A lot of people thought those boys were dodgy—and they could well have been, but from my experience, that's just a characteristic that people use to tag people with who have money. The boys were probably running the family bar or had inherited it over time, or something similar.

Plenty of interesting things went on there, including when a chef spat in a burger and an employee kicked a customer in the head. I might add that neither of these styles was one of mine, but I found it entertaining to know that it was the way of others.

I think the night that stood out most for entertainment, for me, was the night we got robbed and I got a gun held to my head. I remember it was Christmas Eve and I'd just got off the phone to my mate to organize a gathering, as you do when you're 18. I was planning on hitting the city, and we did, although before we could, I had to clean and hose the bar.

While I was in the middle of those jobs, the old bloke working down in the bottle shop ran inside from downstairs and screamed for help. I thought it was a prank 'cause his glasses were all over his face, his shirt was ripped and he was usually a prankster—and his case wasn't helped by the fact it was Christmas Eve.

It wasn't until he screamed, "Please!" that I budged. He wasn't the sort of guy to say please. That's when I ran my backside outside and saw the old robber legging it down a dark alleyway and my man yelled, "There he is! Get him!"

On seeing this shirtless character with a big eagle tattooed on his back, I think, *Shit ah, tough guy …* I've just been training unbelievably hard to try play rugby union with a top Sydney team, I'm at my usual weight of 13 and a half stone, I'm 5 foot 11 tall and I'm pretty fit, so I love having the opportunity to chase the silly bastard down and tackle him.

I catch the guy quick, 'cause he's old and on his last legs for running. Just as I arrive at this clown, within a couple of meters of him, my stupid workmate yells, "Watch out! He's got a gun!"

Nice one, idiot! Why would you tell somebody, "There he is! Get him!" and not mention he's got a gun until I've reached him? Anyway, this robber turns around, and I'm waiting for the gun, but I get smacked over the head with a bottle of wine. Bloody lovely, that was, but at the time, I thought I'd been shot, 'cause I didn't see the bottle; I just heard the bang in my head as the bottle hit.

While I'm smacked out on the ground, this big getaway car's revving its V8 directly in front of me.

I'm gone here—this bloke's gonna run me over!

Then the driver drives off on his mate, the robber, who's standing there alone pointing a gun at my head, shouting, "Stay down or I'll blow your fucking head off! I'll blow your fucking head off!"

I thought, *This is it.* I forgot that people had a weapon to do a robbery. I've had weapons around me before, but not since I was a young kid, and I don't associate them with a robbery because I've never been involved in one. As I've said, I was "green as" and fresh out of the country—18 and clueless.

He doesn't blow my head off, and we later find that the gun this man was holding, in this dark alley, was a replica.

Bloody hell! I thought I was doing the right thing by getting hold of this bloke, but it turned out I got in the way of the boss's insurance claim. They didn't thank me, because they could've claimed $7,000 on the tills if I'd let him escape with no money and only his bottle of wine. Actually, the wine wasn't going anywhere, because he broke it on my head.

Oh, well: you live and learn; *think before you act "He-man."*

It was only the first legal year for working in a bar, so not many young blokes are gonna know the underlying issues of an insurance claim. I guess that incident was a little intro into a money loophole, and I must say I still hit the town with my mate once my police report had been done.

Did I claim compensation as the victim of a violent crime? No: I was too proud and worried about keeping my grandfather happy. We didn't do things like that, in his eyes. That wasn't what we did; we were proud country people, apparently. It was quite a transition, moving back to the city, because I'd been countrified. I was a city kid up to age 11, but had been back and forth from the country over the years.

I was a bit of everything. In Tamworth, I was sometimes called a wog, because I had a sprinkling of Maltese blood, and in the city, I was as Australian as they came. I was born in the country before the old man moved the old lady to Sydney and left her stranded with a couple of us bastard kids ... I was a bit of a "Nowhere Man." There wasn't too much city-style activity during my previous "Suburban slum" years in the poorer parts of town, so I was a fish out of water this time in the city.

I had a funny way of finding my feet, but I had some laughs along the way trying to find them.

I think one of the funniest things I ever saw, and it was around the time of the robbery, was the day my mate fell out of the back of my pickup. He was a funny guy, a friend from school in Tamworth, and loved to smoke a bong. He was living in this big-ass house of one of Australia's richest property developers. He was a carpenter for this guy's company, and because my mate's family were respectable people and friends of the developer's family, he got the job and got to live at their residence.

That home would've been the best house in Hunter's Hill. It backed on to the Sydney Harbour and had the works: swimming pool, tennis court, boathouse and more. This silly mate loved a party, and a bender wasn't at all unusual for him. One day after a bender, my mate was found passed out in the boatshed of this waterfront property, with the door of the boathouse open to the world, and he'd obviously been trying to get the boat out while blind drunk. He was asked to leave the property and because I had a pickup, he asked me to help him move.

We'd packed all his stuff in the back of the pickup, and it was time to go. After packing the pickup, however, we discovered we had no rope! We'd just finished loading in this tip-top TV unit his brother had put together at work, as a cabinet maker, and it was bloody heavy, and worth a bit, too. His bro had gone overseas and asked him to look after it, so we were now looking after it.

We looked at each other, and my mate, Jack, was stoned after having a bong before the trip, and I said, "Okay, Jack, you get in the back and hold all the things together; I'll drive slow. One knock on the side of the pickup is 'slow down!' Two knocks is 'fucking stop!'"

We're cruising all the way over to Maroubra, about 40 minutes away, and we've almost arrived. We've done the busy shopping Oxford Street, and things are looking good. We pull up at the set of lights, pulling into the street of our new rented flat we've organized because we're both now working. This is where Jack's belongings are going.

As I pass the lights to turn right, giving way to cars, I hear a bit of a rumble in the back. There's a slight hill as I'm turning, and it's actually a "no right turn," but I think, *It's sweet: we've done the hard bit.* And I do the corner nice and slow.

When I first hear the rumble in the back, I wonder, *What's going on back there?!* I yell to Jack, "Mate, what's happening?!" And then I hear this big bang. I can't see out the back, 'cause the pickup's chock-a-block.

I ask, "Jack, what's happened? You gonna knock, or what?"

Shit: he's not knocking!

I look in the rear-view mirror, and in the middle of the traffic lights I've just turned right at, this beautiful TV cabinet's on the ground, looking very buckled.

I can't work out why Jack's not knocking. Then, the cabinet starts moving around, and in the middle of the road, and in the middle of the traffic lights.

Holly shit, Jack's popping his head out of the TV cabinet! Oh, shit, I might've killed him! We're off to the hospital, for sure.

Luckily, he stands up and I see his stupid sunglasses, all bent and buckled. They're like something out of *Top Gun*—very "fighter pilot," and not the coolest, and I'd never known how to tell him.

I look at him about 30 meters back and think, *What's gonna happen here?!* I think he'll have the biggest shits ever...

But we look at each other, and man, I'd never laughed so hard in my life. There are people at the lights, looking so shocked. They can't believe what's happened: "country meets city." They must've been thinking, *Look at this hick in the pickup with all the crap in the back... Oh, he's doing an illegal right turn! Oh, the light's gone red!... Oh my god: all the stuff's fallen out... Get stuffed: they've smashed a very nice cabinet!... No: it's moving, and there's somebody—or something—getting out of it... Is he gonna die?... No way: they're laughing!*

We then get the scraps off the road as soon as possible. I'm happy that Jack hasn't died.

When we get back to the house, only another 50 meters from the site, I ask Jack, "How the hell did you wind up on the ground, out of the pickup and in the bloody cabinet?"

He explains that he'd smoked some joints before we left. We'd got to Oxford Street, and he'd thought he'd better get in the cabinet so the cops wouldn't bust us. You see, the cabinet was big and had a section for an old box television with closing doors. The section was raised up from the base, about 60 centimeters, to allow for videos, or whatever, underneath the TV. So, Jack was sitting up high and therefore making the cabinet top heavy on the pickup's side gate, and when I hit the corner on the hill and turned into it, the TV cabinet toppled out.

Unbelievable. I've seen a lot of funny things, this one's got a top-two ranking on my list and has been on it for years. We went straight out after that, talking crap and drinking at some party. Happy days: Jack was alive, and I was finding my feet in a blessed little part of Sydney.

Blue Smartie

4

Dude, where's my pickup?

My university life went on for about four and a half years, for a three-year degree, and I did a diploma for one and a half years before that at the local college. The original diploma was more of a stepping stone to get into university. I didn't know it then; I never knew I'd be going to university—I didn't have good enough grades from high school.

After doing the diploma course for a year and a half, I'd achieved good enough qualifications to do a university degree. That was exciting; I'd become a determined little bastard.

"You can't go to university, Gaston," my mother said. "University's for people with money." I was on the phone to share the good news with her. When she said this I looked to the sky with anger for what the world had done to my mother's mind

For pricks with money! Why am I different?

After hearing that, I became more determined to finish university.

During the first week of university, I moved from Sydney to Wollongong, with all my belongings in the car. It was the first week of the course so I had everything I owned in the vehicle, since I'd just arrived in town. That wasn't too bad until I returned to the car to find it'd been stolen. Everything I owned was in it ... It was a pickup, and an old, beat-up one at that. I'd parked it near the university, thinking I was in a nice town. I'd been at university for the day, and I returned to the pickup a few hours later, but when I arrived, the thing was gone.

It's not that bad; it was just that everything I owned was in it. Also, it was the first week of university, and because I hadn't had enough time to organize myself due to a late surprise of an unexpected university offer, I had nowhere to live. I'd just applied, not thinking I'd get in. Since, I was disorganized I was sleeping on a friend's sofa at his place near the center of Wollongong. I didn't want to be a hassle, so I was leaving all my things in the pickup with a cover on its back. The only stuff I had out of the pickup was enough to fill a small sports bag, which I'd left inside my friend's house.

When I got back to the pickup and discovered it wasn't there, I knew it was gone, but couldn't believe it, and I didn't know what to do. I remember I looked down and that I was wearing a friend's shirt he'd got from one of his relatives. It was a shirt that had a motto on it for the relative's insurance company: "Insure my things." Damn-straight: *"Insure my things."* But the problem was, I wasn't insured for theft.

Now, looking back, the story doesn't seem so bad, but at the time, it seemed that the worst thing in the world had happened. After that, I literally had nothing, and I remembered hearing Mum say, "You can't go to university, Gaston: university's for rich people." That sentence was what carried me through on that occasion. I thought of it and said, like, "Fuck: that fucking car needed new tires, anyway. Those pricks are gonna have to buy new tires." And the car was also heavy on fuel, so the theft had happened for a reason, and the reason was I had stuff-all cash for fuel and repairs.

Thankfully, I'd just been talking to a rugby union team not too far from university and my friend had told them I was a good player and I'd played on representative teams. They luckily called me straight after the incident. That was a coincidence. I was stuck for words. "Someone stole my car, and if you want me to play, you're gonna have to come and pick me up," I said.

They did, and we had a little meeting. They gave me $1,500 in cash so I'd join them, and I was back on track. *Let the good times roll.*

For some reason at the time, I got addicted to getting an education. I loved analytical things, so I was hooked on doing my science degree and proving my mother's thoughts wrong. I don't know whether I was doing the right thing or not, but I do know I kept myself away from bad people—or at least from people who didn't have the vision to succeed in life, and I needed to remove myself from them because I'd been exposed to that type of person over previous years.

I also think that type might've been easily attracted to me. I played sports for all of my growing years, and during that time, you can be introduced to people from all walks of life. That's the one thing about sport: you're all there for the same interest, but you could all be from different socio-economic backgrounds. I couldn't see it at the time.

I was lucky I was introduced to education, and I could thank my first girlfriend for that. She was an educated young lady who'd attended arguably the most exclusive girls' school in Sydney, and for some reason, she didn't mind a piece of Gaston. I didn't mind, for that matter, either: as a horny young man, I was quite happy to offer my services.

I remember that my nan was happy when she met this first girlfriend. She didn't meet many of my girlfriends, just the ones I stayed with for a little while. I was 18 when she met this first girlfriend, and I remember people in the family being worried I mightn't be able to be close to women due to some of the things that'd happened to me. I couldn't see what they were talking about, because I loved my nan and treated all my girlfriends with as much respect as I'd give her. When I was with my first girlfriend, I was clearly head over heels at having a missus, and I treated her as a very close friend.

She was a good girl and she was a lot like my grandmother, but I was a young, distracted male and she was four years older—and a pretty girl too. She wasn't daft, and I'm sure she could see the risks associated with dating this young chap.

We'd been dating for a couple of years, and I was preparing to start university in another town, so we'd finished by that time and I'd been getting ready to explore the world a bit more. During my time with her I learnt that many "normal" people went to university or at least had some sort of direction by doing a course or something similar. That was part of the system, and in order to be accepted by the system, you had to be doing something acceptable in it.

Obviously, the poorer areas I'd lived in had a different system, but stuff being part of that; that was full of ugly, crap-talking people who'd pinch the eye out of your pecker if you weren't looking.

During my time dating this girl, I also moved up in the world, to a more elegant bar in Sydney city's center. While I was working there, I observed that all the better-off kids working there seemed to be involved in some sort of study. Everybody at that age was talking about studying or some course for their careers. So, I applied for my college diploma, my stepping stone into uni—"Bob's your uncle!"—*I* was studying, too.

That's about when I started to appear "normal". I was hanging out with normal people and not ever really considering doing too much bad; I still did—it was still in my blood. It was just petty things, to eat and pay the rent. I'd been doing it since I was a young boy, due to my observational learning.

I learnt how to be a mild arsehole at a very young age. My father was an arsehole who went on to do jail time—I'm not sure what exactly for or how many times he'd done time either. You could say I had the potential to carry on being bad, but that I'd opted not to. It was a bit of a transition, trying to shake the ways I felt were inside me, but I can honestly say I've never done too much bad, as a result of not wanting to upset the man who'd given me new life: my mother's father, my grandad.

I still had certain bad people from the rougher areas of the city who wanted to be a part of my life at this stage, though I was being led to a new light. I still had a friend I considered a good one, who was from Macquarie Fields. He was a real rogue, I tell you—always in trouble and wanting to punch somebody out. I don't know whether he could help it or not; his mother had been only 14 and on heroin when she had him and had given him up during his younger years.

Everybody has a story; you find that out after talking to anybody. It doesn't matter what the extent of the story is, it's all relative to the person's mental capacity. You're only as big as the things that affect you. I was getting to a point where not much could affect me.

It wasn't an easy gig, chipping away trying to get that degree, with little cash. I didn't want to repeat history and be an arsehole like my father or his family. They'd done jail time. Actually, my brother did a bit of time in the end. While he was serving close to one year, he found one of our uncles—my father's brother—in there. A nice little family reunion—how lovely.

I didn't know why I thought I needed to avoid that pattern; I was lucky and helped because of something. It was a gut feeling I had. A lot of people in this world have shown me how to become scum, so I know exactly what not to do. It seemed nobody in my family had any formal education, so I was really led there as a result of my gut feeling.

Sometimes, I think it was more than that; sometimes, I feel as though my uncle who'd passed away was watching over me. It seemed so obvious sometimes; things used to always happen to me on a particular date that were amazing and, for some reason, they coincided with the anniversary of his passing. It's as if he died on that day and was being reborn in me.

I always received a sign from him. After years of struggling, I eventually graduated as a Bachelor of Science. The day I was awarded the degree was the anniversary of when he'd died, and I felt something at the time, too. In the very near future, something incredible was to happen so I'd be able to buy my first apartment in one of Sydney's most exclusive areas—paying cash. The settlement of that property and the receiving of the keys also happened on that anniversary date.

This was the new me: I had opportunity, my own apartment and an education. I was becoming a normal person. I was fit, due to all the sport I loved, and I kept society happy by getting that education. And all of a sudden, I'd satisfied those funny bastards in the system by having assets. Life's funny: I still had the same soul as that young pikey Gaston, but I'd now met society's criteria.

5

Karma

In 2003, I met a Jewish girl who came from one of Australia's wealthiest families. I noticed that members of the Jewish community acted rather strangely around her because of her family's success and the size of their fortune.

I was 23 at the time and still had nothing, but for some reason, she liked this little city man and his countrified ways. She was right into fitness and image, and because I was a rather fit chap who'd started trotting around the healthier parts by this stage, she didn't mind a slice of what I had to offer.

Her family had everything, and they weren't just millionaires; I'm sure they'd gone well past that milestone. I learnt a lot from the way this girl conducted herself and the way people acted differently around her. She didn't seem to fit in anywhere. It wasn't her fault she had money;

she was just born into it. Some people could see that she wasn't the most street savvy when it came to considering others' situations; all many people could focus on was her family's wad of cash.

Her family were very normal apart from the fact their assets were the best of the best. They had high-rise apartments in the city, and I mean they owned the entire blocks. And they owned office blocks as well. They had plenty of other things, from hotel chains to who knows what else.

Something I noticed about them was that they never did anything bad to anybody—they didn't need to. From what I saw, they only did good, and her mother actually always seemed to be helping somebody, by building a school in a Third World country, or similar things I'd occasionally hear at the dinner table. These were acts of generosity that the family didn't advertise.

This way of behaving was very different from the lesser, poverty-stricken ways I'd acquired while growing up, learning from scumbags that good guys don't move forward. If that was true, why did I only observe those twits struggling?

With this family, one thing I noticed by accident was that they never seemed to have too much bad luck. This was something new, and so was the harm-free life they led. I dated this girl for about two years, and I think it was about one year too long, to be honest. But I can see what I gained from the experience.

I remember going away for a few days to Byron Bay with this girlfriend, for New Year's Eve, and the time had come to make a New Year's resolution that would lead me to change my life. I'd been with this girl for some time, and I was young and dumb, and thought she could be the girl I was going to be with. My New Year's resolution that year was "Don't be an arsehole!" I quoted it to myself, and that was it: "Don't be an arsehole!"

I used this resolution to cover everything, and I mean everything. For about the first month after, I felt I couldn't do anything: I couldn't yell out the car window; I couldn't tell somebody to piss off; I couldn't refer to people's unfortunate characteristics; I couldn't take advantage of my build and overpower people, I couldn't even bloody litter—and that one was tough, because I was walking around with rubbish in my pockets all day, due to the fact

I couldn't find a bin once I had the litter to get rid of. I couldn't scratch my backside without thinking about the New Year's resolution. It's one I stick to, and it's been the reason behind changing the way I act throughout life. It all started as a result of knowing this girl and her family.

The real reason I actually listened to the resolution and stuck to it, though, was something that happened to me on the first day after I'd made the resolution, the 1st of January 2004. At the time, I was stuck in Byron Bay with not a penny. It was supposed to be a holiday. I didn't have the heart to tell this girl I had no money. She had plenty of it, and that was none of my business. She didn't give hand-outs; she'd been taught very well how to handle the scabs. I wasn't one of them, and so I kept the fact I had nothing to myself.

I was stuck in Byron Bay with very little, and a bit hungry, too. I remember going to an ATM—a cash dispenser—and trying to get money out, and I knew I didn't even have 10 dollars in the account. That was a problem, because 20 dollars is the minimum amount for a transaction so you can pull money out of that hole in the wall. I thought I'd give it a go and that by some chance I'd be wrong that I had no money, and a twenty would hopefully come out.

I was at the ATM by myself. I think I'd lost the missus 'cause it would've been embarrassing to not be able to withdraw money because of insufficient funds. When I got to the machine, I read the screen before I put my card in, and the message was "Do you require another service?"

Hello, what have we here? I thought. *I haven't put my card in yet.*

There were various options after pressing "Yes," but the thing was, I hadn't seen anybody at the ATM before me, and it was very strange that I was being tested on the first day of my New Year's resolution.

I've got no money and I can possibly pull a load of this money out of this bank account. Somebody's left their card in here and left without it.

But there'd been nobody at the ATM before me!

"Don't be an arsehole!" was this voice in my head.

I had no money.

Okay, I can do an account balance and pull out all the cash ... No: that'd be being an arsehole ... Or I can just calculate what I need to get me back to Sydney and a bit of food to eat before I get paid at work.

I calculated the cost of a cheap bus ride back to Sydney and a couple of days of eating mince, and decided to take out $60, because I knew of a coach that could get me back for under $40. This was seriously scratching to survive. I know it was still being an "arsehole," but I told myself I'd be helping the person who'd left the card in the wall not to leave it there again, and the other thing: I hadn't even seen anybody. It was like a sign to make me recognize my resolution and a little bit of luck to go with it.

A series of things happened over the next few weeks to remind me of the resolution, and it became evident that this was the way forward. I was normally a man without luck, and the way of thinking that nice guys don't move forward was clearly not getting me anywhere.

A couple of days after I'd arrived back in Sydney, I was in my bar job. By that stage, I had about a measly $3 in my account and nothing in my pockets. I was just trying to stick to the New Year's resolution. In the past, while I was working in bars, if I'd been hungry, I'd taken enough money out of the till to buy me some food until I got paid, or if I was short. I couldn't do it this time, and I was bloody hungry.

The first shift back at work, I found a wallet with $15 in it. The old me would've taken the $15 and given the wallet back, justifying the decision as a good thing because the person had his wallet and anybody else would've taken the money. This time, I tell myself, "Don't be an arsehole!" and I repeat the quote to myself when the owner of the wallet enquires at the bar. I give it back to him with the $15 in it, bearing in mind I've got sweet nothing on me.

The owner of the wallet appreciates my honesty so much he pulls the $15 out of the wallet and gives it to me. *I didn't even have to steal it.* Holy shit: this was so strange, but I had $15 on me and enough for food until the next day. Two lucky things had happened to me, and that was almost good enough.

The next day I went to work, I was hit with a real tester 'cause I'd nearly spent my $15 and I was once again left with about three big ones. This time, I find a wallet with $450 in it. That was so much money to me. I was on a roll and these things didn't usually happen. I thought, *No, that's it: you can't be an arsehole, and that's it. This guy's getting his wallet back.* I remember hiding the wallet in my pocket and telling the other bar staff, "If anybody comes for a wallet, I have it."

The manager asks me for the wallet.

I say, "No, mate; I'm giving it to him." I know that the manager would've taken the money, and I want to see the guy's face when I return it and to experiment with whether he'll give me a reward.

Sure enough, the owner comes to the bar, and with all his friends. There are about eight of them, and they're all Irish. This is my test. I give the wallet back with all the money in it and wait for my reward, having a little chuckle to myself and thinking, *Yep: there's a 50 coming my way.*

The owner of the wallet and all his friends can't believe I've given back everything while working in this stinking Irish pub. I clearly can't be working there, because I'm loaded—that's for sure. His friends say, "Give him a reward—go on: give him a reward," in an Irish accent.

Yep: 50, I think to myself, and this scabby bastard puts his hand in the wallet and pulls out a 10 New Zealand dollar note. *You tight prick: what am I gonna do with that? I think; it's almost two-thirds the price of Australian dollars, and where the hell can I spend it?*

"Okay, bud; you keep that," I say. "You just pay the favor forward: you just do the same for the next person." I liked the idea of being "Mister Nice Guy" for once, and I somehow developed the theory that everybody does their bit to make the world a better place. I don't know how, but I started to like the feeling.

So, yes, that Irish man was a tight-arse, but over the next week, I got lucky somehow. It wasn't to do with money; more about something simple a 23-year-old would enjoy, and I felt it was to the value of $450. Because I wasn't so lucky financially, I felt that the "pay it forward" idea had become a reality; it was something like having some mad jeans or clothes given to me and I didn't have to pay for them. As a young guy, that's all I would've wanted to spend my cash on anyway.

Over the next six months, I stuck to the New Year's resolution. I remember I didn't get lucky immediately, to the point I was a "lucky man," but I remember getting less unlucky. That was fine, 'cause somehow I'd convinced myself I had bad-karma debts to pay off. How that got in my head's beyond me, but during and after those six months, I became progressively luckier and things were different. I never did a bad thing by anybody after I'd made that resolution. I do think this is the main reason I'm lucky now, because I had the option to be very bad: I'm smarter than your average criminal, and I have bad blood. I know how to do bad and really affect people, but the point is I don't.

About 18 months later, after an escalation in my luck, my mother tells me she's won the lottery. What on earth am I supposed to do? I have no choice but to not be an arsehole now. I tell you, I've really used this resolution to prevent myself from doing some bad things, and to change my life. I'm now the luckiest person I know, and I rarely meet anyone luckier.

A short time after all this, I was introduced to *The Secret*. Now, I never knew the details about this theory in the past. I was very critical of everything, including that. I've never been to a forum for it. When I say I was introduced, I mean I remember a lot of people were talking about it and I was thinking: *that's kind of like my mind.* I've been so positive since I found karma. I just believe and it happens, now. Anything's possible, and if it's out there, it can happen.

An addition of my own that I found is that you have to give to get. This isn't just with financial stuff; it's just doing your little bit to make sure your section of the world's going to plan. Help an old lady to cross the road, or don't do crap that'll cause inconvenience to someone else, including people you don't know, because it's that crowd you never expected anything from in return. If you want to make a difference in your luck, it's up to you; step up, commit and change your life, so it points in the direction of good.

This isn't all studied for me; it's from practical experience of how I believe I got lucky. You can never hurt anybody. You're responsible. You choose your destiny.

Blue Smartie

6

New shoes

I'll never forget the day Mum called me up to say she'd won some money. At first, she didn't tell me how much we'd won – I just thought she'd won enough to take herself on a holiday and have a bit left over in the bank. I guess that's what you'd assume if your mum phoned you to tell you she'd won some money.

We'd always bought scratch cards and played small gambles when I was a kid, but they didn't pay well. I remember we got a $2 win here and there, but as time went on, we seemed to win even that amount less frequently. Nan did win a $50 once, which was good, but this win with the old girl was massive, to say the least.

I think that when she originally phoned me to tell me about the win, she didn't tell me exactly how much because she was a bit scared to talk about it over the phone. We all found out shortly after, when we were at my brother's home for a family gathering.

What do you say when something like that happens? The timing was perfect, too. I'd just finished university and used my degree to get myself a job. The car I had was about to die and was as embarrassing as could be, but was a requirement for the job I'd landed upon graduation.

When you win the lottery, you don't really know what you're supposed to do. You have all the numbers, and the newspaper in your hand, but you don't have any money yet. You start thinking about how you'll get the money and who you're supposed to ask to tell you how to go about getting it. You become very paranoid, especially if you're living in one of Sydney's poorest, most crime-stricken areas, as my mother was.

If any of those bastards in the area had known my mother had won, well, I'm sure people would've been trying all sorts of things to get their dirty paws involved. We'd hit millions—an eight digit million, too.

Going from poor to that rich is something very difficult to explain. It's not just one transition you need to make; you have to face plenty of new obstacles, because people swarm in like flies on rubbish and from all directions. It was obvious that this bit would happen, but to the extent it happened, and among the people who it happened to, well, let's say you soon saw a business side to them.

We were all trying to keep as composed as possible. We actually didn't tell anybody when we found out we'd won. My mother asked my brother and me to check that the numbers matched the numbers in the newspaper. There were numbers everywhere—a big paper full of numbers, and I didn't know what was going on with it all until my brother pointed out we'd hit the big one.

At that point in time, we were still bloody poor. Mum had to go to collect our luck without losing it or being robbed of it, or something. Some time over the next few days, Mum visited the office where she needed to be, and my brother escorted her there. I thought it'd be best not to go with them, because my sister and brother and I were already involved, and being the oldest, my brother was the man for the job.

A series of things happened over the next couple of weeks before my mother received a big, cop-that deposit in her account and each of us was shopping for a three-bedroom apartment in our desired location. This was a pleasant change, I must say, after living in dumps forever and always worrying about life and where it was going.

I always worried about my mother; she seemed to get tangled up in some knots, for some reason. This time, somebody had shone a big light in her direction. This was a massive blessing. I felt I had nothing to worry about: I had an apartment and a car on the way, and my mother was to be safe forever—or at least that's what I thought.

Over the next couple of months, my backside was sitting in a bloody nice car and an even nicer apartment in Sydney's Bondi Beach. I always get a smile on my face when I think of that time: I had everything—free living, a car, a flat mate who gave me a weekly donation for spending, and a bloody good job. In society's eyes, I was no longer a scumbag. I met the criteria, and I possibly had something that people or vultures would like.

I worried about my little sister, at the time. She was young and still living in a bad part of Sydney when the win came through. Mum put her and my brother in a good area, not too close and not too far from me. That little sister of mine had been through some stuff, and sometimes I don't know how she pulled through.

It's funny what money can do. We'd all been doing it tough before this blessing, and now we were really just over that fine line between pleasure and pain. I can't believe how much we were helped by the energy, or why we were even chosen, or why we were put through all our crap at the start to have this event happen to us.

You start to wonder about life. You start to wonder why things exist, and you think that if something exists, it's possible it can happen to you. After now living in different parts of the world, including cities by the water, I've occasionally heard people who live by the water say, "You've got a better chance of winning the lottery than getting eaten by a shark, so don't stress about getting eaten by a shark in the ocean." *My family's already won one lottery, so I'm stuffed if I'm staying in the water too long any more.* I get in the ocean, but anything's possible in this world, and not much can surprise me these days.

When we won, I remember thinking *I knew something like this would happen.* I just thought, *Life can't be so bad that nothing good happens.* I felt it; it was something inside me, and I wasn't as surprised as much as you'd think I would be at the unbelievable news. When we won, I just thought, *Well, stay focused for the task ahead, and keep a level head.*

It happened to me when I was 25, and the timing couldn't have been better: I'd finished university, alone, and given myself respect for having done so, and I had the impression I could do anything from there—and then this: a bit of assistance. It's amazing what you can do with that assistance. I never knew that life could be so easy when you didn't have to pay rent.

Mum never gave us too much physical cash—not a huge chunk; she was too sensible and didn't want us to get messed up in the head. My sister was young and the windfall could've been dangerous for her future, and my brother was an expert at getting himself into trouble. I remember he was always dazed and giddy, trying to get through life as best he could in his twenties. We had it tough, growing up, and he wasn't coping with things the way we were. Thank God we got rich, 'cause all our behinds were saved, and that's a fact: "No money, no honey" in this world.

Life started to get really interesting for me at this point. I was bloody happy, and I started to see the world as a real joke. All of a sudden, I was considered a different person from the one I'd been all my life. Yes, I suppose I'd been a scumbag in society's eyes before this, but I was now being accepted, and I thought it was a joke.

I recall when I was shopping for my new car, I had to drive my complete piece of junk around to the dealer's yard. That car was the biggest bucket of scrap metal ... I couldn't kill it, though. I'd named it Scoupey. It was a multi-colored, beaten-up Korean S Coupé that had a couple of broken lights and a missing rear bumper. It had cost me around 300 quid.

I'd been pulled over that many times in that heap of junk 'cause the car was always full of defects. I'd always continue driving it because I'd never had the cash to get the repairs done. I had to get to university and driving that bomb was the only way I could get there: I wanted that degree, and I'd stop at nothing for it. I had no money for the train—or petrol, for that matter, or at least not to fulfill all the work and sport commitments I'd signed up for. That's when I had to become a "petrol runner:" pull up, fill up and drive yourself out of there, with dodgy number plates.

I'll never forget one night I was pulled over in that bomb. I thought nothing of rules back then. I used to drive that car everywhere with parts hanging off it and ready to break down, and the rest. On this occasion I was with a "good" friend, or at least I thought he was at the time.

He's with me on this night because we're driving the car without paying attention to society's system. We were off to play sport on that night and we'd been pulled over, as my number plate was reported, as I'd paid my car tax with a bouncing check. I'd forgotten the check'd bounced as it was for the compulsory insurance aspect of the registration; this usually took a few months before the insurance company communicated with the roads and traffic, so I thought I was being hit with more car defects. We were treated like the biggest criminals; the cops mentioned they'd been looking for a car like mine that'd been reported doing break-ins in the area. It was a bit of action, I suppose you could say as a young guy, getting roughed-up, cuffed and leant over the car's bonnet, while looking at your mate. I recall hearing one of the cops say,

"If they move, bash 'em." That was pretty funny, too, actually 'cause I quite liked the idea of being roughed-up by a pack of pansy cops, but we'd had no intention of moving or aggravating any problems. Anyway, we get locked up. The cops interview me, 'cause I'm the man in trouble—it's my car, and me driving. My ex-mate loves the experience because he knows they've got nothing on him and this is his chance to feel like a *Mafioso* in a cell. He doesn't care that I'm about to get hit with the book.

I give my interview, clear myself of the robbery connection, and give them a whole spiel on why I desperately needed to drive the car that night and how I'd had no idea about the bouncing check. Then I say, "At the end of the day, you're just fining me because I'm poor and I didn't have the ready cash to pay the road tax." My car was impounded, and a number of events happened that are all related to being flat broke, and it all escalated from there.

If I'd had money, I wouldn't have been doing a thing wrong, just driving my car, like the people with money. It was true: I was being fined for being poor. Those rules are limiting for the poor. How could I listen to all the rules when the people who made them weren't on my side? People are prevented from doing a lot of things because of the rules. One rule is that if you don't have much money, you don't get too much, and it obviously applies to a lot of people, and at the time, it also applied to me. I was pulled over with all the irregularities I've mentioned—and a few more. I was treated like trash.

This was often the case when I drove that shabby car, even on the day I was going to buy my new car; I always got some real interesting looks, and that day was no exception. I'd found the new car previously and organized with my mother to meet her at the location to pick the car up.

On the way there, I was treated like a crim, as usual. I was driving this hunk of junk on the motorway to pick up the new car and a pack of cops pulled me over. I didn't know they were pulling me over 'cause the car was playing up and wasn't even going to make it to the motor dealer. It was blowing smoke and starting to stall on the motorway, and I think it was because of old spark plugs and leads that were overdue for replacement. I used to pull over and adjust them from time to time, when the car was running badly.

The time had come when I had to do this on the motorway, on the way to the dealer. I was trying to pull over. During that time, a bus full of police officers pulled over alongside me, and I jumped out of the car to pop the hood. I assumed the cops were pulling over to help me, because they're called public servants, after all.

This cop pulls his gun on me. What the...? My car's just broken down, I've pulled over, and now a cop's pulling his gun on me and he says, "The best thing you can do is get in the car, sir—get in the car, real slow."

"Mate, my car broke down."

"Get in the car."

I'm speechless. I think they'll also catch me for doing petrol runners, because I'd done a few drive-aways during the year and heard nothing about them. I'd been doing them with dodgy number plates but thought my time could have been up. I wanted to do stuff legally. I hadn't done that many runners. I just did a few runaways, as I wanted to get to university and still continue my sports. The fact I had little cash wasn't catering for this.

Luckily for me today, the Old Bill hadn't received the news about the shifty petrol runner.

Then, the cop walks up to the car and says, "You were on the phone, back there."

"Hey? My car was breaking down."

"You were on the phone!" And he writes me out a fine for talking while driving, throws it at me, and storms off. It seems he's had a terrible day. I'm a bit confused and pissed off because I wasn't on the phone, but it's all good because of the warm reminder I give myself that my mother's just won a huge load of cash and I'm on the way to pay cash for my new car. So, I get the car back on the road and go to get the new wheels.

It was such a good car, and boy, I got treated differently in it. People actually thought I was something. I was the same, though, those idiots; it was just that I had a smooth ride now.

Shortly after the motorway incident, I bought my new apartment in Bondi Beach, one of Sydney's most exclusive areas. That was fantastic; all I had to do was rock up at the estate agent's and say, "I'll take it!" I went back to their beachside office about a week later to pick up my keys, wearing a no shirt and a pair of board shorts. I felt so good and that there was no need to pretend we had money, because, I guess now, we kind of did.

This was a new life. The day I got the keys for the apartment was my lucky date, the anniversary of my uncle's death. His dying obviously wasn't the lucky bit; I was only 11 months old when it'd happened. I believe he always watched over me after that, and I'd always received signs of luck associated with that date and the number.

Not long after I'd settled myself into my sweet pad, I started looking around for a flat mate. After conducting interviews with pretty women from different parts of the world, for a short time, I eventually had two Italian girls move in. That was sweet. If anyone criticized me, according to society's criteria, I was a young landlord and close to "Bachelor of the Year."

These Italian girls came in, and after living with me for a while, they asked whether their friends could stay in the flat for a couple of days, and the next thing I knew, the place was loaded up with six Italian beauties. No sweat off my back, 'cause two of them—actually, three—were stunning. I was a young, dumb-ass Australian who had no knowledge of the butterflies that awaited him across the pond from Australia.

I'd been working on one of the *Italiana amigas* for a week or two, and when things finally went my way, I thought she was something special. I don't know what it is about those Mediterranean women for me, but they get me going. I think it's in my genes, from my Maltese ancestors, and as a result, when I see those women, I want to eat them.

I followed that beauty to Italy to find, when I arrived, that she'd become a completely different person from the one she presented when in holiday mode in Australia. We weren't able to hang out, then. I was young and just thought the thoughts in my pants.

A quality I've picked up in my life is: if I say I'm going to do something, then I do it; if say I'll get on a plane and fly to the other side of the world, then I'll probably do it.

If you imagine you're walking on a bush trail for ten minutes and you reach an unexpected small creek, what do you do? Some turn back; others step through it. To me, twenty hours of flying is a small creek.

It's a good thing the split happened in Italy, 'cause for me, that country had some beautiful things. I think I got over that one beauty in about 12 hours and went to explore the country. That place had plenty to offer—plenty of amazing historical buildings, detailed statues, streets and lanes, and who knows what else. That was about the first time I realized there are plenty of nice fish swimming in the sea and that the ones I like were near the Mediterranean.

During my time in Italy, I discovered it was a little piece of heaven, and I'm looking forward to the next time I visit the place. It's loaded with detail, from architecture to women and beautiful coastlines.

I remember that by the first time I was there as a young bloke, my interest in the Latin countries had grown very strong. The first year that this fortune happened for my family, it was a pleasant, life-changing experience. When I returned to Australia, I still had Italy on my mind, along with the new sights I'd seen in the world. I had a great job and not much on my mind other than happiness. Not many people could be that happy—I'm sure they can be; I just didn't really know it before my financial position changed.

I remember that for the first time, when people were taking my photo, and I was asked to smile, well, I really was smiling as hard as possible. During the time I spent working in Australia I felt *I'm not paying rent, and I'm used to paying it, so I should have an investment.*

I managed, with the help of a friend, to buy a house in Newcastle, two hours north of Sydney, with the plan of renovating it and making some cash.

I didn't really know the "mate of a mate" too well; I just assumed he'd want to make some cash as well. It turned out he had a hidden agenda, which was for me to assist with the funding of other investments he was in the process of making a mess of—he bit off more than he could chew with the banks. We split up our partnership and I learnt a good lesson about a person's business personality and how it differs from their everyday personality.

I learnt a lot from this character—not from him personally, but from having my solicitor deal with his. I think that right from the start he just thought I was loaded and I could help him. People just assume this—they don't seem to recognize that I actually didn't win anything; my mother did. Maybe, to some, this means they get rich automatically, 'cause most people's mothers spoon feed them all their life and they never get to know what happens when you really win the big one. For my mother and my family, she was helping us in the best way possible: she bought us the essentials; a roof over our heads, and transport.

In my eyes, I was rich—I lived for free and had a bit of income from flat mates, plus I was working. Mum had a good strategy to keep us all level-headed. Anyway, this business partner, if I can call him that, eventually discovered that I, personally, didn't have millions in my back pocket, and as a consequence, we split as partners. I was to finish the renovation alone and move forward.

It was a nice change in my life. I ended up doing about four renovations, and, with the capital I'd created during those renovations, and owing to luck, I got out of Australia as soon as I could. Eventually, I was able to commit to my renovations and throw in my other job. That job was beginning to be a pain 'cause I was making more money from my renovations and could be a real person while working in my scrappy shorts.

I was never into being fake, and that became very evident when the family bumped into some cash. The fact that certain people now talked to me who wouldn't before wasn't only a joke, it was upsetting to think that the old me had missed out on certain things. There was also the fact that nice people are out there who miss out on certain contact in society because of money. It could be worse: I could still be broke.

It was amazing, the new friends I acquired and the stories that ended up going around. In the beginning, I told only a few people. I didn't want anybody to know or think I was a rich prick who didn't relate to other human beings. The people I told couldn't hold their tongues. It wasn't their fault; I think it just preyed on their mind that I was so lucky. Once again, they mostly disregarded the fact I hadn't won and that it was my mother who had.

I guess that's funny: watching people's minds overrule them. It was a joke, but the fact that I couldn't handle the joke also became my flaw; something I needed to control and pull back in line. That's not something you prepare for when you think of getting loaded, so I guess it's part of the new game. In the end, I didn't want anybody at all to know, because it seemed to bring new friends who were all focused on the same thing. They all wanted to hear stories about the luck and what was happening with the fortune.

I remember people coming round and asking my mother for money all the time. This included so called big-wigs who worked with the corporates in the city and many whom my mother never saw near her before our family got lucky. My mother needed help over the years, and these pieces of work were nowhere then. Perhaps they thought they were sophisticated and doing much better than my immediate family. And that might've been true.

All of a sudden, different lunches and dinners were prepared for my mother, and I could see they were all part of a strategy of trying to get paws on some of my mother's fortune.

I'm sure my mother's been confronted with all sorts of issues since this blessing. I know she's lonely now, at times, and very cautious with people. Although the luck sorted out many of her problems, it also gave her new ones. One thing it gave her was the opportunity to find out who could really care for her, without introducing a business side.

I recall once, before the win, visiting Mum's apartment while I was driving my old rundown car and still doing university. I remember her saying with so much passion, "I wish I could help you all. I just wish I could help you all." When she said it, I stopped and thought about it for a moment.

Wow, I guess she does.

I'd never actually stopped and thought about Mum helping us before. I really just always thought her hands were tied in helping herself, and never expected anything from her financially. It wasn't that long afterwards that she got lucky.

Mum often went to church and prayed, and the rest. She always told us to do the same, but I always thought I was praying just by never hurting anybody and being a decent person.

From the very moment Mum got lucky, she had new people around, and a lot of professional advice from people who were nothing and people who thought they were qualified to give advice. The fact of the matter is, she's not making sandwiches in some corner store any more, or doing some little job like that, and to me, that's the most important thing. When it happened she was confronted by people sniffing around—"Hi! Here I am, just popping in to say hi!"

Mum's been hit the hardest by all this, and I'm sure she has a story in her own mind. I've heard plenty she's had to deal with due to her accidental celebrity status. It's been frustrating to hear about all the new residents in the viper pit.

I recall that after she'd won, an old, deadbeat boyfriend of hers reappeared from out of nowhere. I heard that certain people had requests, such as that they needed money for a new business or so they could pull the old one out of a mess and try to regenerate it. Mum had to turn down some people, and naturally, they couldn't put themselves in her shoes and appreciate that she couldn't say yes to the world.

I believe that some people came back and that Mum had bought a close friend a car. It's never ending, I'm sure, and I wouldn't even know the half of it. Mum's living her part, and she's not stupid. I'm sure she doesn't want me to know half of the deadbeats she deals with from day to day. She seems to still have them around—bloody parasites.

Mum's lonely, though, and needs company; I'm sure she can see the big picture. It's unfortunate that she sometimes gets a lot of anxiety, but she's been through more than all of us have. In reality, I'm a lucky man for this. Mum's been put in a position and been the face that's had to deal with everything.

From the word go, she's had a financial team and all the professionals advising her which direction to go in. They've opened up work opportunities for themselves and whoever their friends were. "Too many cooks spoil the broth," I believe my nan used to say. Mum can see the big picture and I'm sure that most of the things that have happened are no worse than half the things she's already gone through as a young woman, growing and learning and single with mongrel kids. There are no flies on her, at least not at the times it matters.

We still have our immediate family, and we're pulling through as best we can. I'm happy that my brother and sister, at least, have company and support in their relationships during transitioning times. After witnessing how much of a gag people can be, and being able to access money so I could head overseas, I did. I wanted to get away and experience a culture I wasn't part of.

Before anybody else really knew about the victory, it was all so simple. Mum was talking about her holidays, and paying off her flat and buying another. We were so vulnerable. As much as it's a whinge, since the win happened, it's been nothing but better times. We just have various new obstacles to tackle. I've done nothing but travel, pretty much, since March 2009—nearly three years. I *have* done other stuff since that date, such as going back to Australia a couple of times to sort out some issues. One thing I had to do was get a back operation, or more specifically a discectomy, from a surgeon, and the other was to sell an apartment I'd renovated.

I made a pretty penny out of that one; it was exactly why I can continue doing what I'm doing now. The other reason I mentioned for a visit home, the spinal operation, was that the surgeon had to do a very complicated operation on an inconvenient injury I'd sustained during my sporting years. The injury had been around for some time and become quite debilitating.

The real reason I'm traveling, though, is money. I love it: it's the best. It lets me do what I do. It paid for my surgery; it pays for my trips. I just hate what it does to people, and because of that, I've been living a secret since discovering its effect on people.

I remember a dream I used to have when I was a little boy. I think the reason I had it was that my family was poor. In the dream, I had lots of sweets in my hand while I was sleeping, and when I woke up, they were all gone. They were Smarties, from memory. I bloody loved the blue ones. While I was in the dream, I remember I had a handful of Smarties and clenched my fist as hard as I could to try to wake up with the sweets. Obviously, I never got them.

I liken this dream to what happened to my family and me. I figure we eventually got the blue Smarties, and it's just a shame that less fortunate people have a problem handling the good luck. I do too, and I need to conquer the problem of not being able to handle that fact that some people aren't able to handle my story. I recognize this, and I'm in the process of getting on top of it.

It must be intimidating for some of the people who once wouldn't talk to the poor Gaston, even though in reality he's carried the one soul all along. This psychological defect of mine is a major cause of my traveling—coupled with my Latin fever and curiosity about cultures.

I originally started my long-term travels in Argentina, in March 2009. That was three years after my introduction, and addiction, to the pretty women who live near the Mediterranean. I started in Argentina, I guess because going there was a good way to escape a world that was my reality.

I initially flew from Australia to Argentina, and that felt the best, and I can't explain why. I was by myself and doing a trip on a budget. I was living in a simple heaven; the place was cheap; the women were beautiful; and the food, cafes, restaurants and nightlife were all the best in my eyes.

And I didn't have to listen to any English whingeing. It's difficult to listen to English gossip at times—things such as "He's doing this!" and "They're doing that!" and "What's it like keeping up with the Joneses?"

When you spend the first part of your life with very little, and you learn to be happy with it and battle along, people see you and they're comfortable with having you around them. You keep battling and striving, you do well, you're happy, and people are still comfortable with your situation. You all go along wishing for the same things. At least most of us do. We wish that one day we'll be able to do whatever we like. We keep wanting, but we never plan for what we'll do if the luck happens—not extensively, because for most of us, it doesn't become a reality. I'm not loaded; my mum is—I learnt how to be a survivor before all this luck happened. I've got beer taste on a Champagne budget.

I've gained a lot, and I'm very happy for this. I've also lost a lot. The one thing I lost that I wasn't ready for was friends. The loss was probably all for the best. I can see it now. You just lose them; things happen.

A lot of stuff goes on behind your back, like Chinese whispers, and the next thing you know, the story's come back to you that you've won the bloody thing. It was interesting to watch the story come back. It doesn't matter how close they are to you; that money just makes people without it go wild.

I ended up playing games with people. I told somebody something and knew I'd told only one person, and I then watched the story come back to me. I was "Flavor of the Month," and the flavor of many unambitious lives. I couldn't be that.

I've found that people will only ever really be concerned about issues related to two things in a simplified life: sex and money. This is a very broad brush stroke, I know, but everything somehow links back to these two issues. If you're a human and you have both of these sorted, you'll be sweet. Just be careful who you tell. People always try to interfere with both of these in anyway they can.

It wasn't a smooth transition.

At the time I had a very pretty Brazilian girlfriend who'd moved to Australia when she was eight. She seemed to be a pretty, articulate young girl who painted a nice picture for me and for the spectators' imaginations. Things didn't work with us, and we went our separate ways. She was a decent girl, but she had her separate issues. And I guess I had mine. I quite liked her and appreciated that she'd met my grandmother, which was a big thing for me. I wanted to stay with this girl, but the man upstairs had his other plans, one of which I can see has been better for me now and possibly her too. If that breakup hadn't happened, I wouldn't have been able to do half the things I've now done. I also don't believe a relationship like the one we had would've been able to withstand some of the emotional stresses I was forced to control.

During my time in South America, I enjoyed being away from all the hassles associated with having a thorough understanding of the conversations going on around me, and I was enjoying my life by taking up new hobbies, such as studying languages, philosophy, literature, Brazilian Jiu-jitsu, and learning about the world. I found myself not wanting to return to Australia. I'd become fascinated with escaping the English world.

Also, my grandmother passed away shortly after my first return to Australia, and that was the time I'd cried the most in my life. I wasn't coping in the English world, and as a result, I had to leave it as soon as I could. Nan's death was so unexpected, and a new can of worms was opened in relation to arseholes, leeches and money. I needed to escape that world and find something I was unaware I was looking for. I'm not sure what it was, but due to my continuously growing faith in karma, I had nothing but belief I'd be looked after.

Hey, Nan,

I just wanted to write to you. I haven't spoken to you in a long time. I hope you're well. I know you know, but I'm in Spain.

This life's gone so funny, hasn't it? You never warned me about all this stuff. How were you to know, though? You made me so strong, and sometimes I assumed you knew everything.

Remember when my brother and I first moved up to

Tamworth? I was so scared to move there. It was because I felt I was out on my own, on the way there. We got the train to your house. You and Grandpa got us from the station, and everything was better from that day on. You did everything for me, Nan, everything, and I miss you so much.

I don't really know what I'm doing at the moment. I'm just living in Spain telling myself I'm learning Spanish. Everything's good. I mean, that's probably the problem: I never planned for everything to be this good. How could anybody?

I wish I could still talk to you. I used to call you every few weeks 'cause you made me feel better all the time. Every time I called you, I felt like everything would be fine just after that. I always called after I'd had a *rough patch. How was anybody to know the patch would be so good now? Not many people can ever deal with the story. I can't tell anybody. That's why I'm talking to you. I'm going to pull through. I know you know. I'm just chipping away.*

Jeez, you were good to me, Nan . . .

Thanks.

I love you.

I know you're busy. I love you. I'm gonna shine, I promise.

x

Blue Smartie

7

Sangria

I had a good experience in Spain when renting a little apartment in Valencia. It was a good little joint—pretty simple, but had everything. The place cost about 600 euros a month and had many Spanish furnishings—a wooden exposed roof which angled up to the pitch in the ceiling; and one of those cool European balconies, which greets a cobbled street. The landlord's name was Angel, which in Spanish is pronounced more like *Anhil* in English. He seemed a caring man in his fifties who treated his apartment as a respected means to make money. I got to live there alone. I'd gone to Spain to learn the *Español*, and I figured that renting a place there wasn't a bad way to do it.

Not sure why I want to keep learning the stuff—something subconscious drives me. I think I was in Spain to start learning Spanish because I wanted to meet the prettiest Spanish women in the world and experience different cultures.

Most days were very relaxed there and consisted of getting out of bed at about 11 a.m., doing a bit of Spanish study and then cruising up to Spanish school. That was my day for about a month. In my spare time I was also studying an English-teaching course online for a few weeks to help foreigners learn English. The logic I had towards doing it was that I'd help myself fund my travels throughout the world, have some new experiences and get to help Latin beauties learn English.

I decided to finish with Valencia after three and a bit months. It was a good little place. It had good people, good prices and pretty girls. I was happy to go, but I also had some fantastic times. I learnt some Spanish while I was there and lived cheaply, eating basic paella, tapas and drinking sangria.

Locals would hangout in historical plazas during the night in the city; it was common to see me in a plaza sipping a one-Euro beer I'd purchased from a street-vending African immigrant and admiring an ancient statue.

I wrote this chapter sitting on a train heading out of Valencia on route for Madrid. I stayed there for one night and then headed to New York 'cause it was kind of on the way to South America, which was the next place I wanted to visit.

I wasn't keen on staying in Madrid too long that time. The place is a bit pricey if you enjoy the finer things in life. Would be good to return, but not until I've cracked the Spanish code. For me Buenos Aires is the promised land— or at least South America is, at the moment. The price is right, and you can buy almost anything you want. I was going there to finish my Spanish apprenticeship and enjoy a few conquests.

While I was in Valencia, I started hanging out with a young French girl who was also studying *Español*. She seemed a bit lost like me. She was a nice girl. I met her and she accompanied me in Valencia for a while.

She seemed to be a nice organized girl when I initially met her. After getting to know her over a couple of months, I discovered she had a different story from the one I'd imagined. I assumed she came from a good family and had a crystal-clear picture. I'm sure her family were fine, it was just that she mentioned that her ex-boyfriend was on the junk. She talked about him often, or at least I could tell she was thinking about him. I later found out that the past two boyfriends she'd fallen for had given in to the chemicals. She seemed lucky, but when I looked at her closely, things seemed different. From a young teen up to when I met her—she'd just turned 25—she seemed to have been with blokes who'd become victims of the chemicals. Her heart was all over the place. I thought about her 'cause I could see she had a good heart, but that part of it was in the hands of a person whose soul was in the hands of chemicals.

I'd been alone for some time by then, so I was I probably thinking beyond things that concerned me. But people can mess you around, and I saw that in her, and it reminded me of the people I'd known throughout my life who'd messed with my program. Always seems to be the case—everybody has a story; people just assume everybody else is near fine. People only get let down when they expect something from somebody and invest time in them as a result.

In Spain, I really had a bit of time to just sit and think. Most of the time, I was recovering from my back operation and living alone, doing minimal exercise—just enough to recover at a progressive pace. I'd come to Spain because I wanted to be in South America to learn a second language, but it would've been too dangerous to recover from a back operation in one of those crime-riddled countries.

Two weeks after my back operation in Australia, I was on a flight heading for Spain. I flew hoping the pain in my back wouldn't get too much for me. The flight was to change over in Singapore, so I thought if it flared up halfway I could step off in Asia. I took the risk and powered through to Europe.

After minding my own business for some time in Spain, and on the other side of the world, I learnt, after my grandmother died, that, for sure, "money is the route of all evil," as she would often say.

The only people in my immediate family now, as far as I'm concerned, are my brother, sister and mother. It's educational to sit back and watch life when you believe in karma.

At the time, I tried not to focus too much on people who lived in Australia. I was in Argentina tasting some of Argentina's finest cuisine. What a place Argentina is: loaded with women, and the dollar to peso exchange rate works a treat. I would've spent a lot less than I'd be spending if I was living in Australia.

But it was interesting the day Nan died. When we were attending the gathering after the funeral, I felt my immediate family pushed aside.

A time of grieving is a time when a passionate person can be scared the most. Things are governed by the imagination and one of the characteristics of the imagination is that the images that shuffle through it are things from a person's past. Beyond this, in order to activate an image in the mind, a person must possess a passion for that memory. It's passion that forces a person to hang on to things. A passionate person may have trouble forgiving and forgetting—maybe a flaw with passion.

I was supposed to be grieving at the funeral, but instead I was learning about humans. As life goes on, a story is written. The present becomes the past and the past becomes a collection of memories. For all of this there's usually an audience—which has either a positive or negative perception—pleasure or pain. As with negative and positive energy, pain or pleasure cannot vanish; they transfer forms from one charge to the next.

Two negatively charged people interacting is a connection which usually results in a negative path. This is why I believe I was helped: I was able to step out of the negative and in to the positive.

We are seventy per cent water. If cold water mixes with hot water there's a mix with a temperature somewhere in the middle. *Play with shit; get your hands dirty*. If somebody wants to sink your ship, it's because they don't want it sailing faster than theirs—pleasure and pain transfer.

Friedrich Nietzsche was a 19th-century German philosopher who believed everything in life came back to "power"—an ability to have freedom. For this, you need money. Negative energy, or jealousy, is the negative person protecting their subconscious from the fear of being harmed by not having power. They're admitting they're not happy with their freedom by emitting negative shots, attempting to bring the positive man, and their pleasure, down so that the negative man no longer feels threatened.

A patronizing person is admitting weakness. They're not comfortable with communicating on a superior spiritual level. They deliver a patronizing blow to bring that level closer to their inferior subconscious state.

My grandmother was the hub that held her family together. When she died that hub was gone. I wanted to be in her house after she died. I wanted to feel my nan's energy, and where she'd once been—where she'd cooked and where she'd given us all love. But my life had consisted of nothing but luck, so I was not permitted to visit.

An understanding of positive and negative human energy transactions is important when you've come from crap, and then bump in to luck, as sentimental ties become your weakness, and a way for those who've experienced pain to have the "power" to transfer some of that pain to you.

Where my grandmother spent her last years was a place I wanted to feel.

"You'll always have a bed here, mate. You'll always have a roof over your head here," my grandfather once said.

It was heartbreakingly educational to know that his words would be pushed aside.

After this, I needed to stay away from Australia for as long as possible. If only I'd learnt to distance myself from those words.

My mother's had many new obstacles since the change. She received great luck, in that she'll never need to worry about money again, but the price she's paid is that she's lost many people.

After spending a few months in Argentina, working on my Spanish and doing my best to live the dream without being disturbed, I decided to go to Brazil, my paradise. It was the smartest thing I could do to treat myself for the human condition of being human.

"Time will heal all wounds," my grandmother use to tell me. At this time, I had to mix those words with my mother's: "everything has a time."

Blue Smartie

8

Your best friend is your pocket

During my five months in Brazil, I had a blast. I did Brazilian Jiu Jitsu there constantly for about three months. It was a dream to be back into it after having back surgery and sitting out the classes for the previous two years. I trained at the best academy in Brazil, and I found it very good. It was nice to have some sort of purpose after being a bit lost over the previous couple of months.

You tend to feel lost when you're transitioning to having a lot of freedom. It's easy to sit back and say, "If I won, I'd do this," but you will find yourself in a transition phase, as your once ordinary life becomes a desired life. The transition is the hardest part of winning and how it's tackled is the key to whether you "sink or swim." Dealing with new issues, which seem simple, can become difficult, as you're accustomed to dealing with similar simple issues, though from a different seat. My mother's had a tougher trot than me. It's difficult to know what Mum's thinking. You get a bad feeling when bad intentions are around. I've seen people around that'd never shown any interest in my mother until the big change in our fortunes.

I've learnt that money can bring out the worst in humans—their business side—and I can only laugh and compare them to the Gollum out of *The Lord of the Rings.*

I've had so much time to think more about how people can be when money's involved. I'm sure I've almost developed an illness that's grown in my mind, making me believe that everybody has a price. I've lost faith in people. I know I'll bounce back. I've been running around the world, keeping my guard up, and all sorts of stuff's happened on my journey—some good, some bad. I've learnt a lot, and experienced a lot.

I nearly died one day recently. I was cruising to training on one of the crazy buses in the hills of Florianópolis, in the South of Brasil, and had a head-on with another bus. There was blood everywhere—it was very scary—I went flying, had to get glass cut out of my legs, got taken to hospital, had to get stitched up, and so on. I recall before I got on the bus, a large line of pretty

Brazilian girls, who were getting on the bus in a lagoon-style fishing village. The bus was heading for the city and the girls were more dolled up than the usual village attire, carrying portfolios, which would pass as résumés and CVs. They must have been heading for job interviews. The ratio of women to men was nine to one.

I carried my jiu-jitsu kimono in a small black sports bag. It seemed logical to sit in a spare seat, at the back of the bus, across from the prettiest girl. My sports bag sat on the seat beside the window. I sat in an aisle seat, across from the girl. I've got my left eye on the bag and the right on the girl. In the upper left corner of my view, the bus driver's handling the steering wheel around tight corners. Then, I see another bus doing the same, heading in our direction. *This bus is going to hit us.* It smashes into our bus—slow motion—slicing up the back half of the cabin, taking out my bag and leaving my kimono to save me. I was sent flying through the air to land in the seat beside the girl, who was now in shock, and screaming at the sight of the surrounding blood-smeared passengers.

As you can imagine, the hospitals in Brazil aren't the greatest—not that bad—but the experience is heightened because of the language barrier, and because of the increased amount of crime, there are people there who are worse off than you.

When the bus had finished crashing, I thought to myself, *Fuck, I nearly died, just like that. I nearly died running from things in my life and I don't even know what I'm running from.* I guess I'm running because I *can* run, at this point.

People can affect you if you're an amateur. I haven't felt like dealing with the new reality back home. In these countries, I've been experimenting with new languages, and because I don't speak them fluently—yet—I don't really have to have a serious conversation with the people here.

For this reason, I guess I'm not taken seriously by them, or at least I never engage in serious talks with them. I think I'm just running from all the vultures' eyes that I'd never had to experience in this world in my past, and while I'm doing it I might as well do it in countries where I consider the women to be pretty. Nobody here knows my story, either—that's pretty good.

Every time people find out my story, they change. For this reason, I haven't told anybody for a long time. The people I last told were ones I kind of didn't think were important to me at the time. If I told people in the past, or at least when I'd gained the knowledge that I could tell them, the only ones I told were the ones I knew I could push out of my life. You develop the skills for identifying these people quickly when your mother wins the jackpot. If you don't, you're going to have a tough time, because the desperate ones soon swarm in.

The Brazilian hospital I arrived in seemed full of people without luck or education, all desperate for an opportunity—and any opportunity, at that. I remember what it was like to feel like that, but I was in Australia, so I had more, but I still had less than most of the people back home. Those days were intense: cruising to university in an unregistered, beaten up car with different-colored panels. Thankfully, I'm out of that situation, and I'm alive from that bus accident.

There's always something happening, at this point in my life. And, unfortunately, a day I'd been waiting for, for some time, also arrived during my time in Brazil. My grandfather really got relief from it: he passed away. It was the 11th of May 2011. I remember hearing him say once when we were sitting together and a frail, elderly man walked past with a walking aid, "Jeez, I hope I don't wind up like that."

Sure enough, he did, and spent time in a nursing home. The day he went into the nursing home was the worst day of my life. I cried like a baby, the same way I did when my nan died. They were days that were equally bad. Grandpa's day was the first, and my first experience of losing a loved one. He was my father, and I was gutted.

The day he died I was in Brazil, ready for the day to come. I think I was prepared for his death because he'd gone into a nursing home first. If he'd just died, I don't really think I would've handled it.

When he died, I thought long and hard about what to do about the funeral. I had time to get back to Australia: my mother had given me a warning he was going to die. My mother said he hadn't been eating or taking his medication during his last four days. I wasn't sure that the reason for the warning would happen, but sure enough, it did.

I got to speak to him about 10 hours after my warning, and he died straight after. The last talk was on loudspeaker with an audience. I was alone in Brazil, but the family heard what I had to say; they were holding the phone to my grandad's ear.

"I love you mate." I cried. "Don't worry, you're going to a better place than here."

My grandad knows I love him. He did a lot for me, and it comes out in everything I do. He did more for me than I'd ever seem him do for anybody. He was denied the opportunity to raise his son because of his unexpected death—at the age of 16. The attention he gave me caused many problems amongst onlookers

I wasn't at my grandfather's funeral, but I was told by my brother he listened to a eulogy that had little mention of us and covered the period up to around the year I was born—1980—with little mention of the years after that.

A lot had begun to happen that year. To be honest, a very bad thing happened. It was during this time my uncle Dan died in the car accident, and this changed my grandparents' lives forever.

It was a coincidence that I was born; I'd been around for nearly a year, and my brother had been around for about two—close to three.

I didn't go to my best mate's funeral because of the human condition and its need for power. It wasn't my fault that my brother and I were born, or that our mother won a ridiculous amount of money. If I'd been there, my memories of the funeral would have been about others. The funeral would've been more about the lives of the living than my mate who'd died.

I thought to myself, *What would Grandpa have done in this situation?* He would've done the firmest, straightest thing possible. So, I stayed in Brazil and let the human condition roll alone. I spoke with my brother after the funeral, and, sure enough, he told me he'd watched other people carry Grandpa's coffin out of the church without him.

I guess this was a simple human way of controlling something—"power."

I'll give him my own funeral in Brazil, I thought.

Over the past year, I've thought myself into a puddle at times. But I've lived a life many people could only dream of living.

I did my time in Brazil, enjoying the culture, jiu jitsu and Portuguese. I then skipped through to Buenos Aires again, on a connecting flight where I decided to stay for a couple of nights. I had plenty of time to think after those days hanging out in Buenos Aires, because it rained every day after I arrived. That wasn't an issue, as I'm always delighted to be a part of Argentina—rain, hail or shine.

I then headed for Colombia, unsure of what the plan was for there. I booked myself in there for three months, but who knows what the stop after that'll be? I had a good time in Florianópolis, and I didn't really want to leave; it was just that it was getting cold. Floripa is good for beaches and beautiful girls, but that was the time of year when those two aren't at their peak.

In November 2010, I purchased my ticket from New York, skipping through Miami to Buenos Aires, which isn't far from the south of Brazil, as a return ticket, because the return price was very similar to that for a one-way. My ticket to Colombia was sitting there waiting, because the return flight was to stop off in Colombia. Happy days, because I hadn't been to Colombia's Medellin.

Hello, Grandpa,

Hope you're well, mate. Thank you for everything you did for me. Was just having a little memory about some of the days you were helping me on the old Holden.

How's Nan? Hope she's good and you're together with your son. I'm not sure whether you're getting to watch too much of my life at the moment, seeing as I'm in Colombia. Anyway, you know you're welcome.

You must be at peace now. Don't worry too much about all the stuff that's going on down here. There are silly people who are just distracted by a life they want a slice of. They failed to learn too much from you. Not much can beat me, and this is just a time I have to get through.

I'm sorry that your time's been consumed by all this, too. You never really got to appreciate the time that was yours due to this.

Grandpa, I'm also sorry I wasn't at your funeral. It was tough deciding whether to attend, though, knowing I'd be heading back there for a potential feud. You know I love you so much, and I think this is all that matters.

I'm living alone and having an interesting life at the moment. I'm not hurting anybody. I know you probably think I should have a girlfriend to keep me in line, and I agree. It'll all fall into place.

Blue Smartie

Thank you for teaching me everything I know. I shine for you. I live for you. I've never done anything wrong since the day you taught me how to be a man. I had a lot of good times with you. It used to be good going to play footy, and grabbing a pie and a soft drink after the games. You were my dad, and it was good to have a dad in you. I couldn't have had a better one. You did everything for me. You were always there. I didn't imagine that that's how other kids would have it, but I guess it is.

It's obvious that some kids have a superior advantage when they're gifted with a good father. I never would've known this if it weren't for you. You were solid, mate. I never met one enemy of yours in my entire life, and there must've been a reason for that. You were a top bloke.

Cheers, mate.

I love you.

Gaston

Blue Smartie

9

Black hole

Living in a little flat at the moment in Medellin, Colombia. *How good it is to have silence.* I've just finished hanging out in an overcrowded hostel for eight days. I can now wash my clothes and organize my things. The apartment's cozy enough to hang out in and has a fridge full of food. I was up on the high-risen top floor today to see a view over the whole of Medellin. The city's the second largest in Colombia, with over 3.5 million people, bordered by amazing mountains creating a valley. I'm in a ritzy area, sitting high on a cliff edge, which overlooks the gully-style city, and poverty just around the corner.

Medellin could quite possibly be a fantastic place to control my thoughts and disappointment in people for a little while. I only arrived very recently, but the place seems beautiful—a nice tropical temperature and green leafy terrain. Small waterfalls gush through the city and the air's as crisp as can be. The place is at 1,500 meters above sea level, which made me lethargic when I first arrived. I felt like I was getting the 'flu until other "gringos" mentioned they were also feeling nauseous from the altitude.

I decided to stay in a hostel for the first week. It wasn't so bad there—nice furniture, renovation, and so on. But some of the stuff that comes out of the mouths of First-World backpackers, I tell you—not all of them—but the hostels do mix a variety of breeds. Some of them are given the cash to go learn about the world from their parents, "Get out of the house! Go and learn something!" I'd say it'd go.

Maybe some get free rent at home so they can save for their trips, which is nicer than putting money aside for retirement or a home.

Not sure what the hell I'm doing in Colombia. I've been told the place is loaded with girls, but I haven't seen any yet, due to the rain. Talk about a trip led by my penis .. . He's getting to know a little bit about the world economy: I've just bought myself a beer and a packet of penicillin, and I only paid $2 for the lot. That's what dreams are made of. They'd easily have cost me $15 back in Australia.

I'm feeling good at the moment, fit due to my jiu jitsu training in Brazil, and I must say I was very lucky to meet my professor down there as my intro back into jiu jitsu. Returning from back surgery and rocking up to an academy, with minimal Portuguese, to do the first session back from that kind of surgery wouldn't be for everyone. The Proffy's got a good academy: It's often full of black belts, and sometimes there's nobody except black belts to roll with—you can really advance quickly that way.

Today was a pretty good day in Medellin—not too intense. Some might call the jiu jitsu training part intense, and it was rather hard today: There seems to be a lot of Colombians in the camp dropping through, and plenty seem to want to rip my head off. I can tell they like me, but they want to beat me. I think they might think I'm from the States—Colombians get treated differently when they need to obtain a visa to visit the US. Aggression on the mats only reinforces that the jiu-jitsu techniques that I'm studying are working. I'm being too nice there, I'm a visitor with manners, and I am still nursing this 13-

month-old back operation. There aren't many contact sports you can persevere with after back surgery—technique is the key to rolling this smooth art, as it's referred to in both Portuguese and Spanish: "Arte Suave." It also keeps me out of trouble. I party less and keep my mind in a healthy mode.

My coach has offered to give me a local tour on Friday. Word has it there's also a character joining us from Denmark to do training, and he'll also be on board. With a little luck, I'll see some local secrets, such as the poorer barrios surrounding the city. These tend to have no foreigners, and if you do see any there, they'll stand out. My Maltese blood keeps me out of trouble on some occasions, but it's clear that I have money in some areas.

When I look back to before five years ago, I see I didn't think of doing anything like what I'm doing now. It's difficult to imagine doing anything like this. I can only thank the energy that's in charge that made it all possible.

I thank my lifestyle for leading me into this situation. In the year 2000, I met a Russian professional wrestler who'd just competed at the Sydney Olympics. He was fit. I'd always thought I was fit, but when I began to train with this guy, and found out more about the crew he trained with, I was soon to discover I needed to train harder if I wished to continue feeling as fit as I did.

This new crew of men became my new comrades and we all trained together for many years after. I can't really complain after coming from many rundown areas in Australia, and suddenly finding myself living and training on an amazing Sydney beach. I couldn't help but believe in karma after that, and the more life panned out, the more it became evident that karma existed. It applies to me right now, sitting in my modern apartment, overlooking Medellin.

I sometimes I don't feel comfortable living "the life." I love it, but sometimes people make you feel funny about doing it. The way some people might be, once they see you in a nice place or discover that you own your own apartment in an exclusive area, or they discover you've been traveling for three years straight, all over the world, and in style. Maybe that's just what I think, because I was such a broke-ass once. I wouldn't really know whether it's "in style," to tell you the truth—maybe it's just "with sense."

A lot of people traveling seem to drop in and out of places at the drop of a hat. That's when things get pricey. When you're always on the move, you need to cover costs for short-term accommodation, transport and amateur moves you wouldn't do if you were familiar with the place. I stay in places for a minimum of three months. That way, I get a good feel for the place and do it in a cozy apartment as opposed to with foreigners carrying guide books in a hostel.

When I was a pikey, some of these sorts of people wouldn't talk to me, but I need to let this go. I should consider how lucky I am and that these people would never guess I was once a pikey—a lot really admire exactly what I'm able to do. I've become somewhat of a travel guidebook. I've become good at the things I want to do—or at the way I live. I find a lot of travelers take notes about how I approach foreign countries.

I saw this happen with a young guy I was living with in Brazil four months ago. I met him in a hostel I'd decided to stay in for a week, on the island in Santa Catarina. I thought I could use somebody to split bills with. It was okay, it was only for six weeks. I don't think I could've done it any longer. I've become paranoid nowadays—convinced people are always sniffing around looking at things that aren't for them. It's like an over-alert twitch in my mind that I deliberately turn down a notch.

I moved myself out after a short while, and I guess living with him was just a reminder that, ok, he wasn't that bad, I was just being shown that that's how people are and I need to accept it—the guy didn't do a thing wrong. I'm starting to recognize changes in myself due to my experiences and the amount of time I've elected to be alone. I find myself in Medellin now, and the place is good, if a bit lackluster. It's still good; I just expected a little more.

The people here seem to be very different. It could be as a result of the way they've been treated here in Colombia. They do get separated from the world with the limitations in education costs, work opportunities, visa restrictions and currency exchange. I'm just a foreigner here: the city's cheap, and the women are beautiful.

I'm here for the next two months. I don't want to change my flight ticket, because I've blown a lot of money changing fares all the time, but let's just wait and see. I think the other reason I'm thinking of leaving, is I want to return to Australia briefly, as I want to be back in Brazil soon. I kind of feel that if I don't start to make money soon and clear a few things up in Australia, I'll probably suffer when I return to Brazil.

I can't just go and ask my old girl for money—it doesn't work like that. Every Tom, Dick and Harry does that to her, and if I was to as well, I'd only put more stress on her or put myself in the same category as them. I have enough to do what I need to do. I don't need much.

Hey, Nan,

Hope you're well. I haven't written to you for a while. I've just remembered Grandpa's died and he's now with you. I hope you're all together.

I've just got my new apartment in Medellin. The place is very interesting. My apartment's clean and pretty good. I'm very happy at the moment because I was living in a hostel the previous week and the place was full of imbeciles.

I guess you've been watching my little life and wondering what the hell I'm doing. You've probably noticed I'm losing faith in people too. Oh, well, I can see it too. I'll try not to let it get worse. I know I have a few little problems to sort out. When I've sorted them, I'm sure I'll conquer.

I wonder what you're thinking of my Spanish. It's coming along, hey? Very funny stuff.

Well, Nan, just thought to say a quick hi. Just sitting in this little apartment. Sometimes I don't really have too many people to share things with. So, you're the person for it now.

Blue Smartie

I'm fine, though, Nan. It's just that I'm now very selective about who I'm hanging around with. You know that people are dangerous. You saw that with the people in my life. I guess we'll see what happens to everybody at the end of the race. I mean, I won't, but you will. I plan to keep well and truly away from negative people.

Just got some Colombian television show on in the background. Not sure whether you're watching it. I remember when you used to sit in the seat late at night in Tamworth and we'd talk and watch TV. You'd have your glasses on and be doing something fiddly, like sewing a button back on a shirt, or something. Anyway, it's a nice memory.

Ok, Nan.

Goodnight.

Blue Smartie

I love you. Say hello to Grandpa for me.

Gaston

Blue Smartie

10

Spilt milk

Over the past few of years, I've managed to learn Portuguese and Spanish, and to select my favorite parts of this world. I'm getting the Spanish to a point where I can meet very nice people, see a completely different world, and almost start a new, meaningful life away from Australia. Still not exactly where I want it, but it's on the way. These are the little things you get to work on when you have less stress—maybe that's why many of the rich kids play instruments and focus on the arts. I've been pulling out the guitar since I've been roaming alone for so long, too, strumming a few beats since leaving *España* about 13 months ago.

There are different sides to the world—different lives, different seats—and some people have it easier than others. An energy decides who sinks or swims. People decide how they deal with either scenario based on the tools they have. Situations can get out of our control when they're new to us, turning life into an emotional roller coaster until it can be a smooth path.

It seems that people with bad luck can have it for a period, and that people with good luck have the option of having it for a period as well. I remember being a recipient of both and the different lives I led during those times.

It's not that I've ever *studied* anything about spirituality or anything related to karma, it's just that when I examine the correlation between the lives I've led and the luck I've received, I feel I have no option but to believe in those aspects of life. I don't know the theory behind it all, just the practical stuff. It seems the more I attempt to identify the problems in my life and resolve them mentally, the only way I can do so is without doing bad. The life I now have is perfect in the eyes of the old Gaston.

I do have to admit that this whole fortune's had a downside, but I'll only see it as the "downside" as such until I've learnt to cope with it. The disappointment I've had from people ... In reality, I should really never have expected anything from them. If you expect something from somebody, there's the probably of upsetting your own calmness. Plan A shouldn't bank with expectations of others.

The positives out of the negatives are that my immediate family members are all closer now, and I talk to my mother every day. My mother needs to know I'm near. If she didn't at least have the people she gave birth to, then I wouldn't know what the purpose of being in this world would be.

My grandparents are now at peace, and I never would've once imagined I'd be able to deal with losing them. I'm able to say this now with peace, and thoughts that tell me that we have the potential to conquer all thoughts—"everything has a time."

Hey, Nan, Grandpa and Dan,

I hope you're all well. I wonder what you're all doing and whether you're together. Maybe part of you is all inside me keeping me strong. I know you always have been, Dan, and I thank you for this. Your love for my mother and my family has pulled us all through, and I thank you for guiding us.

Grandpa, I can see you smiling now you're with your boy, and you're probably doing a little boxing stance and tapping him on the shoulder with a smile. I'm glad I could give you some enjoyment throughout life.

I think about the family we once had from time to time—I was looking at photos online the other day—and Nan, you were right "Money is the root of all evil." It splits up people who in reality need all the support they can get.

I promise I'll never hurt anybody for being too human. I'm sure they'll recognize that what they've done they'll one day have to reflect on. I'm in the *process of eliminating all my anger and recognizing that these times are the human ways for testing the route we take when we're opting for our bad or good destiny.*

It beats the hell out of me how I even think like this. I think it all started from you, Grandpa, telling me I could never steal from anybody because somebody, somewhere along the chain, was paying for it. I'm sure you told others the same.

Thanks for your continued support and for being a part of my life. I love you all, and I'll never let you down.

Love, Gaston

Everything has a time.

Blue Smartie

Gaston Cavalleri also wrote and published *Crystal Caviar*.

www.ingramcontent.com/pod-product-compliance
Lightning Source LLC
Chambersburg PA
CBHW031622040426
42452CB00007B/632